Payday Loan Business Start-Up

How to Start a Payday Advance Lending Business

Be a Cash Advance Loan Broker to Help People Borrow Money When They Need It Most: Includes Marketing Advice

By

Ben Henry

Copyright © 2020 – **CSBA Publishing House**

Email:csbapublishing@gmail.com

All Rights Reserved.

No part of this publication may be reproduced, stored in a retrieval system or transmitted in any form or by any means, electronic, mechanical, photocopying, recording or otherwise without the proper written consent of the copyright holder, except brief quotations used in a review.

Published by:

CSBA Publishing House

Cover & Interior designed

By

Jennifer Rothschild

First Edition

Dedication

I dedicate this book to God for the inspiration to write this life-transforming book. I also especially dedicate this book to you, the reader, for buying it and taking the time to read it to acquire knowledge. I hope you find it meets your satisfaction.

I wish you the very best in your new business endeavors!

Contents

Introduction 8

Definitions of Industry Terms 11

Chapter 1: Understanding the Payday Loan Business 15

    The History of Payday Loans 17

    How Payday Loans Work 19

    How to Get a Payday Loan 21

    Risks Associated with a Payday Loan Business 31

    Avoiding Risk 35

    Skills Needed to Start a Payday Loans Business 36

Chapter 2: Establishing a Payday Loans Business 39

    Picking a Business Structure 40

    Why Choose an LLC 43

    Setting Up a Limited Liability Company (LLC) 47

    What's in a Name? 52

Chapter 3: Initial Research and Due Diligence 66

    Collect Customer Data 66

    Conduct a Feasibility Study 72

    How to Conduct a Feasibility Study 77

Chapter 4: Understanding Financial Terms with Payday Loans .. 89

    Calculating Interest 89

    Understanding Loan Fees 90

    Understanding Gross Profit 91

    Understanding Net Profit 92

Understanding APR 92

Chapter 5: Business Investment Requirements 96

Startup Costs 96

The First Three Months 103

Finding Startup Funds 105

Chapter 6: Researching the Right Commercial Locations 111

Demographics 112

Security 113

Accessibility 113

Cost of Rent and Utilities 114

Competition 114

Potential for Growth 115

Other Nearby Businesses 115

Chapter 7: Create a Business Plan 117

Benefits of a Business Plan 118

Types of Business Plans 119

Components of a Typical Business Plan 120

Marketing Plan 127

Financial Plan 136

Chapter 8: Legal Matters 138

Restrictive States 140

Hybrid States 140

Permissive States 141

Federal Guidelines and Regulations 142

Consulting a Lawyer 147

Chapter 9: Employee Matters 153

Chief Executive Officer 155

Loan Consultants 156

Administrative/Human Resource Manager 156

Marketing and Sales Executive 157

Accountant 158

Customer Care Representative 159

Company Handbook 160

Chapter 10: More About Marketing and Advertising 162

How to Create Your Payday Loan Business Website 164

Search Engine Optimization (SEO) 169

Launching an Affiliate Site 170

Affiliate Tracking Software 173

Payment Arrangement for Affiliate Marketers 174

How to Find Affiliates 175

Advertising Strategies 180

Advertising Channels 183

Chapter 11: The Payday Loan Process from the Lender's Point of View 196

Basic Loan Requirements 197

Bank Account Validation 199

Creditworthiness 200

Affordability Assessment 201

Financial Responsibility 202

Reason for Borrowing 202

Honesty 203

A Borrower with No Active Bank Account 203

A Borrower with Bad Credit 205
A Borrower Without Employment 206
Payday Loan Repayment Terms 209
Conclusion 211

Introduction

I was born in Bloomfield, Indiana, to business-oriented parents who owned separate businesses. My mother operated a laundry business while my father was a pawnbroker. He conducted his business from a storefront not far from our house but sometimes would do so from the house. I was an only child and spent most of my time with my father. As a result, I became curious and interested in the pawn business.

As a pawnbroker, my father provided secured, short-term loans to borrowers in exchange for items of higher value as collateral. One day when I was about 19 years old, a disagreement occurred between my father and a locally famous musician. Many people in the neighborhood sided with the musician against my father. The hostility affected the whole family, and in the process, I lost friends.

This incident changed my perspective about the pawn business. I wanted my father to close down the shop, but my influence wasn't convincing enough. I decided to research other friendlier money lending ventures he could pursue.

I read about many money lending business alternatives, but the payday loan business stood out. I carried out a feasibility study and shared the results with my father. To my surprise, he embraced the idea and soon took it up. That is where my payday loan business journey began. 26 years later and with three payday loan businesses to my name, here is the story of my journey and experience in the industry.

This book offers a guide and secrets on how to start your payday loan business and turn your capital into a lucrative venture. To make the most of this book, read carefully through every page while taking short notes for later reference. I would also encourage you to continue your research and read everything that you possibly can get your hands on about this business. Knowledge is power, especially when you're entering into a brand new business venture.

Definitions of Industry Terms

Annual Percentage Rate (APR): The interest rate and fees on a loan expressed as a percentage for the whole year.

Broker: A person who negotiates transactions between lenders and borrowers.

Check Advance Loan: A lending method that requires the borrower to provide a postdated check for the loan given.

Collateral: Valuable asset a borrower provides as security for the repayment of a loan.

Collection Agency: The company hired by lenders to collect payment on unsecured loans that borrowers have defaulted on.

Credit Check: The act of reviewing a borrower's credit score and history to assess their record on debt repayment.

Credit History: Record of a borrower and debt repayment plan.

Credit Report: A report showing a borrower's credit history used to determine their creditworthiness.

Credit Score: A score showing a borrower's likelihood to pay back the debt. It is used to determine the risk of lending money to the person.

Creditworthiness: One's ability to repay credit.

Debt: Money owed to a lender.

Default: The status of an unrepaid loan within the stipulated time.

Electronic Transfer: The direct transfer of funds from one account to another.

Finance Charge: Interest paid on a payday loan.

Interest Rate: A percentage representing the financial cost of borrowing money.

Internal Revenue Services (IRS): Federal government agency that regulates taxes.

Lender: A person or entity that provides money for borrowing.

Payday Loan: Short term loan issued with the expectation that the borrower pays it back when they get their next paycheck.

Payday Loan Late Fees: These are fees charged when a borrower doesn't repay his loan on time.

Personal Loan: This is an unsecured loan for personal use.

Postdated Check: A check whose validity date is sometime in the future.

Power of Attorney: A legal document permitting the holder to act on behalf of another.

Principal: The amount borrowed less interest and loan fees.

Term: The duration from the time of lending to the time of loan repayment.

Unsecured Loan: A loan that does not require the borrower to provide collateral.

Usury Laws: Laws that cap APR.

Chapter 1: Understanding the Payday Loan Business

Payday loans are a short-term, unsecured loan where the loan's principal is a portion of a borrower's next paycheck based on his earnings. The borrower is usually required to provide the following documents:

- Identification such as a state-issued ID, certificate of citizenship, passport, or a driver's license.

- Proof of employment or reliable income, including the previous three months of pay stubs, bank statements for the last three months, employer's contact information, or some other proof of income if self-employed.

- Proof of residency, such as a recent utility bill or copy of their lease or rental agreement.

- Finally, the borrower may be required to provide personal or professional references of people who can attest to the borrower's strength of character or who can vouch for their employment.

Payday loans provide relief for cash-strapped customers to fulfill a temporary financial need. Payday loans generally run for 14-30 days, depending on the terms or how often the borrower gets paid. The loan is intended to be repaid upon the borrower's next payday.

The History of Payday Loans

Payday loans are not a new phenomenon as we can trace their history to as far back as the 5th Century. People have always needed quick loans. Hawala was the first concept of fast money lending method from person to person. Hawala is a system or agency for transferring money traditionally used in the Muslim world, whereby the money is paid to an agent who then instructs a remote associate to pay the final recipient. The term comes from the Arabic word "ḥawāla," literally meaning "assignment, bill of exchange." Lenders and borrowers banked on trust without which the whole system would fail.

Later, banks formalized money lending services. Bank loans were, however, only accessible to the wealthy and the well-connected, thus, leaving out a majority of people. This led to the birth of pawnbrokers, who provided secured short-term loans. Borrowers were required to provide a valuable item as security against non-repayment risks. If a borrower failed to pay back the loan on time, the pawnbroker would sell the security item to get back his money and profit. There were instances, however, that the pawnbroker was not able to sell the item and would end up incurring a loss. The introduction of check cashing systems, a money lending method where borrowers gave lenders postdated checks in exchange for money, minimized such losses.

In the 1980s, after decades of strict regulations, restrictions were relaxed in the banking industry. People could open bank accounts and potentially access personal unsecured loans. Access to these bank loans was still a challenge to many because of the loan requirements. Payday loan businesses emerged to cater to the financial needs of such people. Payday loan businesses cater to mostly

When my father and I started this business, technology was still unpopular. Walk-in clients who came to the store for loan processing were the main clients. Today, this industry has gone online and even embraced text message transactions. Borrowers use Google to find us. They can also apply for loans through our website, get approved for the loan, and receive funds via direct deposit to their bank accounts or phone transaction services. Most borrowers prefer online transactions because they are discreet, safe, and they receive their money within minutes.

The payday loans industry continues to evolve and establish its place in the credit market. In 2019, about 12 million Americans took out a short-term, high-interest personal loan like a payday loan. This industry has been on the rise ever since 1947. It is depression and recession-proof, meaning that even during times of hard economic downtown, short-term personal loans will always be in demand.

How Payday Loans Work

Payday loans function differently from other money lending facilities. This business provides loans to two kinds of people: those who urgently need money to help cover immediate cash needs before their next paycheck, or those whose paychecks can't last them to the end of the month.

Payday loans are usually small amounts of money to a maximum sum of $1,000 repaid in a single payment on the borrower's next payday. For security, the lender requires that the borrower produces either a post-dated check or authorizes an electronic bank transfer. The repayment amount includes the principal of the loan, interest, and loan fees charged. Most payday loan brokers charge interest of between $15 and $25 for every $100, for a 14-day loan period, and 5% of the loan amount as fees. The interest and fees make up the profit gained.

Clients receive approved loans immediately or within a few hours either in the form of cash, check, or as a direct deposit to their bank account. When borrowers are unable to repay the full amount, the lender allows them to pay the interest and the loan fees, then renew or rollover the loan into the next month.

Payday loans are known to charge steep interest rates because of the short repayment periods and the strict usury laws. However, these loans are becoming increasingly popular and widely appreciated. Here are the reasons consumers choose to partake in payday loans:

1. Despite the high-interest rates, borrowers find these short term loans easy and faster to access.

2. Lack of alternative financing options due to poor credit ratings.

3. Fear of borrowing from friends and relatives.

How to Get a Payday Loan

If you're looking to enter this business, you have probably been on the customer end of a payday loan transaction at least one time before. To help you understand the product and service you are offering with your new business, here is an overview of the payday loan process from the customer's point of view. Towards the end of this book, we'll examine the same process from your side as the lender.

A payday loan is meant to help you meet an urgent financial need before your next payday. The payday loan, just as the name suggests, is a loan given against a postdated check or authorization of account withdrawal on your next payday.

When the loan repayment date is reached, the lender either banks the check or makes a withdrawal from your account using the postdated check.

Application Process

The requirements for a payday loan vary from one lender to the other, but the most basic are:

a) You must be at least 18 years old

b) Have an active bank account

c) Provide proof of employment or a reliable source of income

d) Valid identification

Your payday loan will not get approved if you do not meet the required criteria. You are advised not to rush your application no matter how urgent your need is. Should it be rejected, that information goes into your file and may affect your credit rating later and, subsequently, your future borrowings. To improve your chances of approval, ensure you meet the following requirements:

The most basic payday loan requirements are that you are employed, have a reliable income source, and providing valid identification. You should also be 18 years and above and have an active bank account where your loan will be deposited and recovered.

Most payday loan lenders will not approve your loan in the absence of an active bank account. Here are two main reasons why you must have a bank account.

a) A bank account presents an efficient and easy way to confirm that you have a regular income, whether you have other debts you are servicing that may affect your affordability and the source of your income.

b) The lenders can schedule your repayments through a standing order or a direct account debit to reduce the chances of non-repayment.

Your creditworthiness helps the lender determine your likelihood of paying back your loan. It is like a measurement tool used to measure the risk of lending to you. A low credit score means you are a high-risk borrower. Either you have no current credit history or yours is a history of late or nonpayment. A good or high credit rating, on the other hand, gives the lender confidence that you will make your repayment. It improves the chances of your application being approved.

Lenders use your repayment history to determine your credit score. You have a bad credit score if you have been making late or missing on your repayments. If you have never borrowed before, you will still end up with a poor rating as there is no proof that you will repay. Your credit score is an indication of the levels of risk that you pose to the lender.

A bad credit score or history, however, does not hinder you from accessing payday loans. Lenders will offer you what is known as a bad credit payday loan, designed to help customers with a bad credit history. Bad credit payday loans are there for those in an emergency or difficult financial situation but made mistakes in the past that negatively affected their credit ratings.

Bad credit payday loans come with very high-interest rates and charges because you are considered a high-risk client. You must borrow within your limits and make your repayments on time to avoid getting into further poor credit ratings.

Lenders will need to verify that your monthly net salary can offset the principal amount you are seeking and have some left to take care of your monthly expenses, such as food and rent.

Most payday loan lenders are not likely to offer you a loan as you cannot provide proof of employment. However, others are willing to loan you provided you can prove certain positive factors.

If you have a good credit history, this can work in your favor. You should be able to show that in recent times, you have recorded no missed or late repayments and that you have been managing your debt responsibly.

If you can provide proof of alternative sources of income, then you can show that you do have money coming in, just not in the traditional sense. Despite unemployment, lenders would like to be assured that you will repay your loan. Your income doesn't have to come from a monthly paycheck, but other steady sources will suffice. Your sources of income should be able to give you money that is sufficient to cover your regular needs and has enough left to pay back your loan.

To qualify, you may also provide proof of near future access to a significant amount of money, such as an employment offer or contract, a signed sale agreement of a real estate or investment property, or an inheritance you are about to receive.

Show personal responsibility by paying off your previous debts to avoid an increasing debt level. The lender may refuse to approve another loan until the previous debts are paid in full. Taking a loan to pay off another loan shows that you are not financially organized.

Lenders use the loan application form to determine your credibility and whether to approve your loan or not. Incomplete or inconsistent information may raise suspicion on your part, and your application will be rejected.

Lenders will inquire about the purpose of the loan and seek to verify your ability for timely repayment. Payday loans are for emergency needs or temporary financial shortfalls. Borrowing to use on long term projects or luxury will be rejected.

Lenders are more likely to approve small loans for a start. You are therefore advised to only apply for what you need and not extras for luxury. You increase your chances of approval by applying for smaller amounts. You can gradually increase your loan borrowing limit with timely repayments.

Customer's Research

Before filling a loan application form, find out who the different lenders are and compare their interests, charges, and repayment policies. Compare the loan features, including the extra amount you will be charged in case of late repayment. Settle on what is most favorable to you.

You can also negotiate with your lender on the interest to be charged. Use your good credit score and repeat business as the basis of your argument.

Compare your lending options. Look for reviews from customers who have used the facility before making an informed decision. You can also consult an online credit broker for advice on the lender with the best interest rates and acceptance.

Consider getting a guarantor to back your application. The involvement of a guarantor reduces your perceived risk, and you can get better interest rates. The guarantor offers the lender a second chance to get his payment should you fail to do so. This means that your guarantor has to be someone with good credit history and meets all other payday loan approval requirements.

Repayment Terms

It would help if you learned how to manage your finances to cover your needs carefully, especially when you are unemployed. However, emergencies and unexpected situations may arise that need the extra money that you may not be able to raise, considering you are not employed.

It is crucial that you repay the loan as per the agreement terms as missing or failing to repay will damage your credit score. Consider taking smaller amounts that you will be able to repay comfortably.

The main aim of payday loans is to provide financial relief due to an emergency before your next payday. They are issued for short durations as you are expected to pay back the whole amount from the next paycheck. Read the repayment terms carefully on your application form. Find out what will happen should you not be able to pay back in time.

In most cases, should you not be able to pay back in time, the lender will roll over the loan to the next month. The other option would be to allow you re-borrow money to settle the previous loan. It is always better to repay the whole amount at once because prolonging the payment period attracts additional fees or higher interest rates.

There is always the risk that the borrower will default on a loan. This may incur added expenses for your business to attempt to collect on a bad loan. In the next section, we'll discuss the risks associated with running a payday loan business.

Risks Associated with a Payday Loan Business

Risky situations threaten the profitability of a business and its continuity. Identifying and understanding the potential risks associated with the payday loan industry and adopting a realistic risk management strategy will help shield your business from the effects of the risks.

Below are possible risks associated with the payday loan business. We will discuss each risk in detail.

1. Credit/default risk

2. Market risk

3. Liquidity risk

4. Operational risk

5. Legal risk

6. Reputation risk

Credit/Default Risk

Defaulters are a big risk to your business. Credit/default risk occurs when borrowers either totally fail to repay their loans or do not repay in time. You can reduce the effects of this risk by charging higher interest rates as compared to traditional lending institutions, conducting due diligence by carrying out a background check on the borrower and ensuring they produce valid proof of employment and reliable income.

Market Risk

Your competition is financial lending institutions like banks and micro-finance institutions and other payday loan businesses. Should any of them decide to reduce their lending rates, your business will be affected. Market risk is the risk of possible investment losses arising from changes in market interest rates charged on loans.

Liquidity Risk

Liquidity is the ability of the payday loan business to access cash to lend to its borrowers. If your business is unable to provide loans to its customers in time or to the tune of desired amounts, you will lose them to your competitors. You can mitigate this risk by forecasting your borrower's needs and creating an easily accessible cash reserve for emergencies.

Operational Risk

Operational risks are losses resulting from errors and inadequate or failed internal systems and processes. Misjudgment errors, internal fraud, or oversights are some of the most common operational risks. You can avoid or mitigate this error through planning and employing qualified and trustworthy people.

Legal Risk

This loss arises due to negligence or misunderstanding of the laws and regulations related to the payday loan businesses. Failure to observe the regulatory requirements, such as filing your tax returns, may result in penalties. Your business may also suffer financial loss and legal penalties due to non-compliance with applicable statutes and internal policies. Seek legal advice from a qualified attorney and accountant to avoid these risks.

You also stand the risk of a lawsuit against you by a customer should you go against your contract agreement.

Reputation Risk

A good reputation boosts your business image. Any news that portrays your business in a bad light will have a negative impact. Reputation risk is the loss of a good business name due to malpractice or criminal activities by the owner or employees. Practicing good governance and business transparency are some of the ways to avoid or mitigate this risk.

Avoiding Risk

These risks are unpredictable. However, there are steps that you can take to minimize the impact should they arise.

1. Identify and analyze the possible risks. While these business-related risks can usually be foreseen, be sure you understand them before undertaking your new business.

2. Come up with a strategy or plan on how to deal with the risks should they occur. I have provided some ways to deal with specific risks listed above; be sure that you have a pro-active plan to mitigate risks as they arise or to avoid them completely.

3. Take immediate action to counter the risks. Amit Kalantri, book author and inspirational writer, said, "Sometimes the loss from taking a wrong action is less than the loss from taking no action." Even if you're unsure about what to do in a risk-assessment,

be pro-active and don't be passive about dealing with the risk.

4. Keep a record of all the actions taken, challenges faced, and the outcome for future reference. Keeping notes of the situation and how it was resolved will better help you prepare for facing that challenge again. Good record-keeping in all areas is a priority, especially when you're dealing with other people's money.

Skills Needed to Start a Payday Loans Business

Like any other business out there, anyone can start a payday loan business. The payday loan business can turn out to be a rewarding investment with proper and efficient management. You need basic and essential business skills. Other basic skills that can boost your business include:

Financial Management

The payday loan business is a business of money where your financial management skills will minimize financial mistakes and help you realize a profit for your business. You should be able to calculate interest and loan fees, forecast your cash flows, and monitor your profit and loss.

Customer Service

You should be able to interact with your clients respectfully and formally to create and maintain a good working relationship with them. Let your customer care services reflect the image of the company.

Networking

There are times that you will need support from other people. Networking by building relationships with other industry players will help you grow your business.

Leadership and Problem-Solving Skills

Demonstrate outstanding leadership skills when handling and interacting with your employees. You should also be able to solve problems and make the right call for your business. Your ability to make the right decisions no matter the circumstances will determine how successful your business becomes.

Sales and Marketing Skills

As an entrepreneur, you will need to demonstrate strong sales and marketing skills to sell and promote your services to attract and retain customers.

Apart from these skills, you also need to be familiar with all the laws and regulations governing the payday loan business. As your business grows, you can identify your shortcomings and employ qualified employees to fill in the gaps.

Chapter 2: Establishing a Payday Loans Business

You can choose to get into this business by building your own company from scratch or by buying an existing payday loan business. To start from scratch means you have to put together everything yourself and have a sufficient lending capital.

Buying an existing business, on the other hand, gives you the existing client base, many of whom will still be your repeat customers.

This book will examine mainly how to start a brand new payday loan business from the ground up. While you may inherit many of the completed steps when you purchase a pre-existing business, you may find yourself re-branding and re-marketing the newly managed business as if it were brand new.

Picking a Business Structure

There are three main forms of business structures that a payday loan business can adopt. The structure that you choose has a great influence on your ability to raise capital and the amount of taxes you will pay. Each structure comes with its own set of paperwork required to complete the business registration. There is also a difference in the amount of personal liability wrapped up in the business.

You will need to decide on a business structure before registering and filing for appropriate licenses and permits. You can seek the guidance of an attorney or accountant before settling on a structure. I will give you the basics to help you make an informed decision.

Sole Proprietorship

You have full control of your business operations, but you are liable for all the obligations of the company. Also known as an individual entrepreneurship, a sole proprietorship is a business owned by one individual without any legal distinction between it and the owner. Raising enough capital as a sole proprietor is often challenging. This type of business structure is more suited to self-employed individuals who most likely won't be employing others to work in their business. This is not as common a business structure for payday loan businesses.

Partnership

A partnership is a business legally owned by two or more people who share managerial duties as well as profits. The partners manage the company together and assume responsibility for its debts and other obligations. This is not as common as an LLC in the payday loans business, but it might be advantageous if you're looking to start this business with another person who can bring you start-up capital. More often, you would still most likely establish an LLC instead of a partnership, but it is an option.

The other business structure is a corporation, which has different types, but that is not very common with small businesses. The taxes dealing with a corporation are much more complicated. For the purposes of this book, I am assuming that you, the reader, are probably starting a brand new business venture from the ground up by yourself or perhaps with one other person. Establishing a corporation would not be ideal in this situation. I would strongly encourage the LLC option as the establishment is easier, and the liability is much lower.

Limited Liability Company (LLC)

This is a business structure whereby the owners are not personally liable for the liabilities or debts of the company. The advantage of this form of business structure is that you are protected from personal liabilities, and in case the business becomes bankrupt or faces a lawsuit, your personal assets won't be at risk. This would be the preferred business structure for most new businesses, including payday loan businesses. An LLC can be managed by one person or more than one person. In most instances, husband and wife partners are normally 50/50 managing partners in an LLC. You can establish how involved each managing partner is in the business, but it is most often split equally.

Why Choose an LLC

It would be wise to have your payday loan business as a legal corporation. Forming your company as a Limited Liability Company (LLC) will protect both your business and personal interests. An LLC offers you limited liability protection as well as pass-through taxation.

Having an LLC as your business structure means that you (and your business partners) exist as a separate entity from the company, and, therefore, cannot be held liable for the company's debts and liabilities.

Pass-through taxation, on the other hand, means, your business income is free from tax at the entity level. However, if you own the business together with a different partner(s), then you will have to complete a tax return for the company. On a personal level, you will be required to report any income or loss you receive from the company in your tax returns and pay the applicable tax.

Advantages of an LLC

1. **Limited Liability**: With an LLC, you and your partners are shielded from taking personal responsibility should the company run into debts or other liabilities. Creditors can only file lawsuits against the company but not you as individuals. Creditors, therefore, have no right to pursue your assets to settle debts owed to them by the company. In a situation where the company is financially crippled, company assets can be liquidated to pay liabilities.

2. **Taxation**: When it comes to taxation, your LLC is not considered a separate entity from you. The

company is not taxed. Instead, you pay the necessary taxes through your income tax as per your tax liability.

3. **Flexibility in Membership**: The number of members of an LLC is not restricted. You can be the sole owner of your payday loan business or own it as a partnership, trust, or corporation.

4. **Flexibility in Allocation of Funds**: If you own the business with others, an LLC offers flexibility in investment and profit-sharing. Initial capital investment is not necessarily a representation of ownership percentage. Ownership allocation can be done through an operating agreement. The same applies to the distribution of profits.

5. **Fewer Compliance Requirements**: Forming an LLC is easy with few state compliance requirements and paperwork.

6. **Credibility**: Most people see LLPs as more credible compared to sole proprietorships or

partnerships. Customers are, therefore, likely to trust your business more.

Disadvantages of an LLC

Forming an LLC has its drawbacks, too.

1. **Initial Cost**: You will pay more to form an LLC compared to sole proprietorship or partnership. Depending on the state you are registered in, you may also have to pay ongoing or maintenance charges, further increasing your costs.

2. **Limited Life**: The life of your LLC is limited by you or your partners' tenure at the company. Transfer of ownership of an LLC is not easy. The company ceases to exist when even one member leaves. Furthermore, to bring in a new member or to make changes in the ownership shares, all the members must approve. However, you and your partners can agree to include such provisions in an operating agreement to overcome these shortcomings.

3. **Self-employment Taxes**: When you own an LLP, you are considered to be self-employed, thus, required to make self-employment tax contributions.

Setting Up a Limited Liability Company (LLC)

Forming an LLC is an easy process, but requirements vary slightly depending on the state where you want to register the company. This section covers the necessary general steps to follow when forming your payday business as an LLC.

Decide the State to Form Your LLC

You can register your LLC in any state of your choice, which could be the state you plan to operate your business from or register the LLC in a different state from where you will run the business. However, to operate your business in a state you did not register the LLC, you have to register it with that state as a foreign LLC. You will, therefore, have to incur extra formation and administrative charges.

LLC formation requirements and taxation vary from one state to the other. Find out which state would be advantageous to register or operate your payday loan business.

Choose your LLC Name

The name you choose for your business needs to comply with your state's rules for LLC naming. Some states have prohibited the use of some names, especially if they are offensive or undesirable. Your legal LLC name should have an LLC designator at the end. The business name you choose should also not be similar to that of another already registered LLC in that state.

We will discuss picking a name at length in the next section.

Create your LLC Operating Agreement

An LLC Operating Agreement is not a state requirement. However, if you own the business with someone else, you should consider making written terms and agreements. It is recommended that you prepare an operating agreement before you start the LLC formation process. The reason being, one of you may not be happy with the terms and decide to opt-out.

An LLC operating agreement is an agreement among you and the other owners on how to manage the business. The agreement should clearly spell out the financial rights and management responsibilities of each member to avoid future disputes. The agreement should also include how ownership transfer or addition of members is to be carried out.

It may not be necessary to come up with such an agreement if you are the sole owner of the LLC. However, having one affirms your existence as a separate entity from the company. You also can have, in writing, instructions to be followed in circumstances where you no longer have the ability to run the business yourself.

Obtain and Fill Out a Copy of LLC Articles of Organization Form

You can obtain this form from your state's Secretary of State office or website or from the responsible department that handles such matters. When collecting the form, inquire about filing fees and any corporate tax that you will need to pay when returning the form. You should also find out whether you will be required to post a newspaper notice on your intentions to form an LLC or a post confirming its formation. Currently, this step is only needed in the states of Arizona and New York.

Correctly complete this form giving all the required information. An LLC Articles of Organization is a simple form without many requirements. Some of the details required in this form include the name and location of the business, the purpose of the company, the registered agent's name and address, and member(s) names.

Submit the completed Articles of Organization Form

Submit this form together with the necessary filing fees and corporate tax (if required). When approved, you will be issued with a certificate or a confirmation document that will serve as proof that your payday loan business is now a legal entity.

Apply for an Employer Identification Number (EIN)

You are required to obtain an EIN. You will be required to use this EIN on the company's bank accounts, income, and self-employment tax filings.

Open a Business Bank Account

Open a bank account for your LLC to separate your personal and business finances. The business bank account is not a legal requirement but separates you as an individual from the business entity.

What's in a Name?

Aside from your location, the right name for your payday loan business has a significant impact on its success. It distinguishes your business from competitors and aids in marketing and branding. A wrong name, on the other hand, could fail to connect with your target market or lead to lawsuits.

Below are the steps to choosing an appropriate name for your payday loan business:

1. Decide on your brand strategy

2. Coin a name

3. Adhere to naming rules

4. Confirm business name availability

5. Register your business name

Decide on Your Brand Strategy

A business usually has two names: a legal name and a trade name. Before naming your business, decide whether or not to separate your legal name from your trade name. A legal name is for formal documentation, while a trade name is for marketing purposes. Sole proprietors and partnerships, however, use their surnames as legal names. Most businesses usually have their legal names listed as their trade name as well.

A brand name, on the other hand, is the name of a particular product or service. For example, if your legal name is "Alabama Quick and Easy Payday Loans of Montgomery, LLC," you may want to shorten that to a trade name of "Q and E Payday Loans." In this case, you might have to file a legal DBA (Doing Business As) declaration so that your business can operate under that shorter name. The shorter trade name would be what the general public would know your business as, what you would list on business cards, and what your sign on your business would say.

You might invent a sales tactic to offer different types of loans. Say that you name one of your loan options the "Alabama Slammer," which offers same-day deposits of the loan amount, hence reinforcing that you are "Quick (Q) and Easy (E)." In this scenario, your legal name, trade name, and a product/service brand name are apparent, but they also carry the idea that your business delivers services fast and applying is simple.

Coin a Name

Use the following suggestions to help you create a catchy winning business name. First, go for a memorable name. Keep your business name simple so that potential customers can easily find you online. In the example above, you can see that the legally listed business name is unique, but it's really long. The shorter trade name is much easier to recall.

Secondly, pick an adaptable name. Choose a name that will not limit you to a specific state, city, street, or geographical location. In the future, you may want to expand to other regions, but your name will not match your expansion plans. This is the downfall of the legal name in our example above. Luckily, the trade name is much more adaptable as it does not limit the company to just Montgomery, Alabama.

Thirdly, pick a relatable name. Your business name should convey a positive and relevant meaning so that people can instantly tell that you offer payday loans. You should probably say specifically the words "Payday Loans" in your business name. Since you most likely won't be offering any other type of products or services, this should be apparent.

While this may seem like a no-brainer, be sure to pick a name that is original. Avoid the temptation to modify or use someone else's business name. You may not be able to register it, and if you do, you may face a lawsuit for copyright infringement.

For example, if in your town, perhaps there is a payday loan business that is doing quite well. It would be your direct competitor for your locale. If that business is called "Sally's Payday Loans," you cannot and should not name your business something as similar as "Sal's Payday Loans" or "Sallie's Payday Loans."

In the days of the phone book and yellow pages, businesses would often name themselves something that would show up first in the listings of their business. What I mean is, in phone books, particularly the yellow pages business listings, the contact information for a business was listed by category in alphabetical order. Consumers would go to the yellow pages and search "payday loans" and find an alphabetical list of businesses. Naming your business something that started with an A, such as "AAA Payday Loans," would place you higher on the list in the yellow pages than perhaps "Bob's Payday Loans."

While this naming tactic is outdated, since the yellow pages are not as common as a source of business referrals, you should still think about getting on the front page of the Google search results. We will discuss SEO rankings later in this book.

When picking a name, think about how customers search for payday loans and where most of your customers might view your business information. We will discuss having an online presence more later.

With that said, you should register your business name's website address. At least, you should obtain a ".com" website domain. Establish your presence online and get a professional web designer to design a unique website. If you don't have the startup funds to hire a web designer or online media specialist to help with your SEO (search engine optimization) keywords, there are several sites that will help you establish and host a professional-looking website.

You could try https://www.wix.com/, https://www.godaddy.com/, or https://www.weebly.com/. You will usually have a small fee for registering your domain name that will need to be renewed yearly. You will also have to pay for hosting. It's not enough to just buy a .com and make a website; someone has to "host" your website, which will incur a fee. If you also want the ability to make online sales, you will also have to pay for establishing a "shopping cart" and interfacing with money handling platforms like PayPal.

There are different options when paying for website hosting. You can get standard hosting, meaning that the host will basically just house your website on a secure connection. You can pay for managed hosting, meaning that the host will conduct maintenance, updates, and upgrades as technology demands it. Managed hosting will be the ideal choice if you don't have someone else to manage your IT needs.

You will also need to consider making your website mobile-friendly, as most customers will have a phone and could easily access your website from a phone or tablet.

If you are making transactions or collecting data on the site, such as email addresses, you will need to purchase an SSL certificate. The SSL certificate puts the little lock symbol in the website address line and assures customers that the information that is transacted on the site is secure. The cost of this security certificate varies.

A good indicator of if your business name is original enough is if you can't find an already established .com of the name that you want to use. Just plug the name you want into a Google search bar and see what comes up. If it doesn't bring up a company website, but rather if it shows something like "this domain name is for sale," then you're probably in luck. Nowadays, nearly any business has some sort of online presence, even if it's just a digital business card.

Another place to check for an original business name is to look on Facebook for a business page of that same name. You can do a quick Facebook search to see if the name you want is already established as a page name. If not, you're good. If so, you may want to consider altering your business name to make it more original. Facebook listings are also a good way to find competitors in your area and what the public thinks of them.

Get feedback and ask others what they think of your business name. Run the name by your friends and family for feedback and suitability. Be sure not to share the name with anyone who you don't trust. Some other entrepreneurial opportunists might steal the name from under you before you get a chance to register it.

Adhere to Naming Rules

There are different naming rules depending on your chosen business structure. If you have a Limited Liability Company, your business name will include the words "limited liability company," or the abbreviations LLC or L.L.C., at the end of your business name. As you may recall from the running example above, the legal name of our fictitious business is "Alabama Quick and Easy Payday Loans of Montgomery, *LLC*."

A sole proprietorship type of business structure strictly operates under the owner's surname or the owner files for a DBA (doing business as) to use a different name. Filing for a DBA is different in each state. Usually, you will have to contact your county clerk's office to request a form and submit a filing fee. A sole proprietorship is prohibited from using words or designations within the name that imply the business is a legal structure, such as, "Inc. Ltd. or LLC."

With a partnership, the partners' surnames must be included in the business name to apply for DBA (doing business as) to use a different name.

Check the Name Availability

Check with the state business database if your preferred business name is available or taken. After confirming its availability, protect the name by registering it with the relevant state office. In most cases, it's legal for you to use the same name as another company not located in your state, but illegal to use the same name as another business registered in your state. An exception to this rule applies to businesses that have registered a nationwide trademark with the U.S. Patent and Trademark Office (USPTO). While name availability is generally only restricted by state boundaries, you'll perform two searches -- one within the state you wish to form the business and one with the USPTO https://www.uspto.gov/.

Register Your Business Name

To make your business as a distinct and legal entity, you are required to register it with state and local agencies depending on your business structure and location. Failure to register your business makes you miss out on certain benefits as personal liability protection, tax, and legal benefits.

Your entity name is the legal identity of your business. This name protects you at the state level, and it must be unique. When you complete the application to register your business, the name that you indicate as the entity name registers your business name.

If you intend to trademark your business name, search the U.S. Trademark Electronic Search System to confirm there's no duplication. Once you are certain that it is unique, you can apply for a national trademark, which makes your business name legal in any state where you are registered to conduct business. A trademark protects your business at the national level.

Sole proprietorships and partnerships can apply for a DBA to use as their business name instead of their surnames. While applying for this kind of registration provides no legal protection, most states require it. This would be an instance where you want to register a trade name, as we discussed in the example of the "Q and E Payday Loans" business.

Engage a trusted website to check your domain availability. If available, register it and ensure you pay to own other top-level domain names to prevent malice from the competition. In case the domain name is already taken, find a way to purchase it from the current owner or switch to a different domain name. Your website domain name should match your business name as closely as possible. In our running fictitious example, I would probably try to get the address "qandepaydayloans.com," if it's available. If it were not available, I might try "QEPayday.com" or "QandELoans.com."

Your payday loans business does not necessarily need to be registered with the federal government to become a legal entity. However, you can register to get federal trademark protection.

On the other hand, you must register your business with the state where your business is located. Do this online, by filing paper documents in-person/mail, or register with either the Secretary of State's office or the appropriate business bureau or agency.

The following information is required for business registration:

- Business/entity name
- Business location
- Ownership or the management structure
- Registered agent information
- Number and value of shares, where applicable

The total amount you could spend on business registration is about $300 or less, but this will vary by state.

Online registrations are shorter and faster compared to physical presentations to the government office or filing by mail. An e-filling process can take at least 10 to 15 minutes if you fill out your paperwork properly. If you present your documents in person at the state agencies for registration, the process will last between 30 to 90 days.

Chapter 3: Initial Research and Due Diligence

Collect Customer Data

Collecting information about your customers is vital to understanding who your customer really is.

Customer data helps you build their profile. From this profile, you can understand and engage them better. Such data include the customers' personal, behavioral, and demographic information.

The right knowledge of who your customers are helps you better understand how to tailor your loans to meet their needs and the effective marketing channels you can use to reach them. Consider the following before you start collecting the data.

1. The customer information that your business will need for decision making to improve your service delivery.

2. The transactional data you will be collecting.

3. How you will organize and keep the data for reference.

4. Data protection laws and the measures you will take to comply.

5. The data collection methods you will use.

6. How you will use the information collected and the benefits it will bring to your business.

Types of Customer Data to Obtain

There is so much customer information that you will be able to obtain as you run your business. To understand this data better, divide them into the following categories:

Personally identifiable information is information that identifies your client, and you can use it to recognize who they are.

Linked information is information that expressly identifies the client without any additional information such as their full name, credit card details, or phone number

Non-linked information is information about the customer that cannot identify them unless paired with other information. For example, you are not able to recognize who your client is with just his first name. However, when the second name is added, you may identify them.

Non-personally identifiable information is anonymous customer information. You are not able to use it to recognize or identify them. Non-personally identifiable information includes information such as a client's IP address.

Engagement data provides you with information about your customers' interactions with your business and their behavior on your marketing channels. Example of such data is the number of website visits and its most viewed page, the number of likes, replies and shares on your social media posts and the number of email or phone engagements you have with your clients.

Behavioral data gives you information that helps you understand your customers' borrowing patterns, such as the number of loans borrowed, amount, and repeat actions.

Attitudinal data provides information on your customers' perceptions, feelings, and emotions towards your business.

Ways to Obtain Customer Data

There are many ways to obtain customer data.

Directly from Customers: Collect the necessary data through the loan application forms and bank details that clients submit at the loan application stage. You can also obtain their data during your one on one engagement with them either through phone calls, emails, or face to face.

Customer Feedback and Survey: Feedbacks and surveys help you gather information on your customers' needs, preferences, and attitudes towards your service.

Website Analysis: Use tools such as Google Analytics to help you understand the demographic and geographic location as well as interests, referral sources, and behavior of your clients when they visit your company website.

Social Media: Social media engagement metrics such as likes, shares, and comments can help you get insights into the sentiments, attitudes, and characteristics of your clients.

Customer Service Software: You can use customer service software to interact with your customers and gather their data during your engagements.

Benefits of Collecting Customer Data

1. You can use the data collected to segment your target market based on their characteristics.

2. The data collected helps you to understand the borrower's needs so that you can tailor your loans to meet those needs.

3. Once you have segmented your target market, you can streamline your marketing strategies accordingly.

Conduct a Feasibility Study

A feasibility study is the evaluation and assessment of a business for its practicability, viability, and success potential. Conduct a feasibility study before starting your payday loan business. It will help you determine the factors that will help you safeguard your investment and propel you to success. Without the right foundation, your business will suffer losses.

I encourage you to carry out a feasibility study before venturing into a payday loan business for the following reasons:

1. To determine if this business is viable and profitable before committing your time, money, and other resources.

2. To understand your goals and identify the kind of business approach that will work best for you.

3. To identify your target market and the existing competition.

4. To identify the essential requirements that you need to have before you start.

5. To predict and identify questions, problems, or risks you may encounter. You can, therefore, prepare how you will handle or avoid the same.

6. To determine the amount of capital you will need to start your business.

7. To gauge your willingness and ability to withstand the physical, emotional, and financial constraints that come with running the payday loan business.

8. To open your eyes to new possibilities, opportunities, and solutions that you may have never thought of or considered.

A feasibility study for a payday loan business usually focuses on the following major areas:

- Market Research
- Business Approach
- Legal Issues
- Financial Analysis
- Marketing Strategies

Market Research

You need to conduct thorough market research before you set up a payday loan business. A properly conducted market research will give you a clear picture of these important factors:

a) A demand projection estimate of the potential market for payday loans in your community.

b) Identifying your target market to define your potential client and assess the potential of the business.

c) Revenue projections to ascertain a realistic and achievable revenue amount.

d) A look at your geography to pick a location that contributes to the success of your business.

e) Competitor information research to identify the local competition, assess their market strength, and realize how to stand out.

Business Approach

Understand your goals about how you want to conduct business and use them to define the kind of business structure that will be best for your payday loan business. Part of your decision making will involve deciding whether to operate from a physical storefront or online (or both) and how much interest you will charge for the loans. In this business, this defines your pricing strategy. Because the price of a payday loan is not like a traditional price on a product, the interest rates you choose become your prices.

Legal Issues

Before you open doors to your business, it is essential that you familiarize yourself with the laws and regulations that apply to the payday loan business in your state. This business comes with many regulations as well as legal requirements. You can seek the services of an experienced lawyer to help you out with things such as drafting a loan agreement for your business. We will examine the legal issues in detail towards the end of this book.

Financial Analysis

Carry out an analysis of your financial parameters such as expected fixed and variable costs, projected profit and loss statement, and break-even analysis. Determine the extent of delayed repayments and loan defaults that you can withstand without your business collapsing. We will discuss how to understand the accounting associated with this business in a later chapter.

Marketing Strategies

Establish an extensive marketing campaign that will ensure maximum visibility for your business. There are various marketing strategies that you can employ to reach your customers. Some advertising ideas include:

- Traditional print advertisements in newspapers, brochures, and flyers
- Google ads
- Word of mouth advertising
- Social media
- Customer reviews online
- Relevant websites and online directories
- Email marketing

How to Conduct a Feasibility Study

Involve the relevant stakeholders and get their feedback and opinions. Ask questions and analyze your data to ensure that it is factual.

Conduct a feasibility study to determine the viability of establishing your payday loan business. You should determine if the business is economically justifiable enough to invest in it.

Your feasibility study will include conducting market surveys and preparing a balance sheet and projected income statement.

For more information on the feasibility study, watch this YouTube video by BizMove called "How to Start a Payday Loan Business | Including Free Payday Loan Business Plan Template"
https://www.youtube.com/watch?v=Nodqq_2x-P8

How to Find Your Target Market

Over the years, the cost of living has steadily risen, but household income has not as much, leaving many people struggling to meet their financial needs. The average American household survives on a paycheck to paycheck basis with little or no savings to cater for emergency needs.

Below is a table showing monthly and annual average American's income and household expenditure.

Item	2017	Monthly	% of after-tax income
Average income after taxes	$55,180	$4,598	
Average annual expenditures			
Food	$7,729	$644	14.0%
Food at home	$4,363	$364	7.9%
Food away from home	$3,365	$280	6.1%
Other food	$1	$0	0.0%

Housing	$19,884	$1,657	36.0%
Shelter	$11,895	$991	21.6%
Non-shelter housing expenses	$7,989	$666	14.5%
Apparel and services	$1,833	$153	3.3%
Transportation	$9,576	$798	17.4%
Vehicle purchases	$4,054	$338	7.3%
Gasoline, other fuels, and motor oil	$1,968	$164	3.6%
Other transportation	$3,554	$296	6.4%
Healthcare	$4,928	$411	8.9%
Health insurance	$3,414	$285	6.2%
Non-insurance	$1,514	$126	2.7%

expenses			
Entertainment	$3,203	$267	5.8%
Personal care products and services	$762	$64	1.4%
Education	$1,491	$124	2.7%
Cash contributions	$1,873	$156	3.4%
Personal insurance and pensions	$6,771	$564	12.3%
Pensions and Social Security	$6,353	$529	11.5%
Personal insurance and other	$418	$35	0.8%
All other expenditures	$2,010	$168	3.6%

Average annual expenditures	$60,060	$5,005	108.8%
Net income / (deficit)	($4,880)	($407)	

This information shows that families are spending about $400 more every month than what they earn. Payday loans offer relief by offering short term loans to such families to enable them to meet their financial obligations. The other target groups for payday loans are:

1. Low-income earners who are not able to meet their monthly financial obligations. These are people whose income cannot last them from beginning to the end of the month

2. People with limited credit options either as a result of bad credit ratings or in situations of emergency, and they need to access funds almost immediately.

3. The middle class who look to live beyond their means.

Understand the Competition

As a business, you have two types of competition: direct and indirect. Direct competitors are straightforward. These are other payday loan businesses in your area. This is easy to find, usually with a simple Google search or maps search for your city. You can instantly know who you are directly competing with because the name of the business will usually include the words "payday loans," "cash advance," or "cash loans."

For our fictitious example business, centered in Montgomery, Alabama, here are the Google search results for "payday loans in Montgomery, AL."

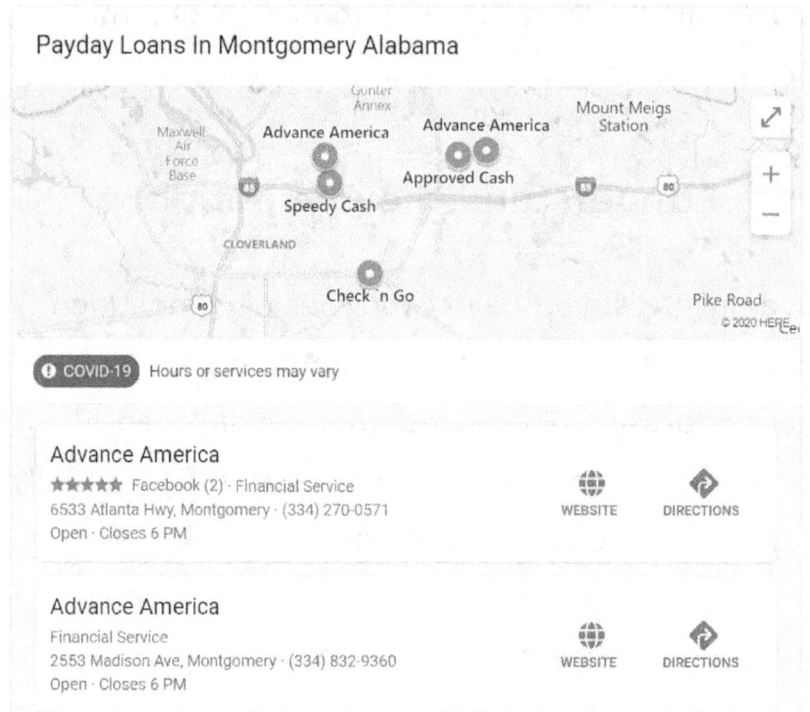

Apart from competition from other payday loan businesses, there are a variety of debt-relief alternatives that your target customers can turn to. These solutions would be your indirect competition. Here are some indirect competitors:

Salary Advance: Some employers allow their employees to request advance payment before the due date of their paychecks. This is not considered a loan as it will be deducted from the next paycheck or series of paychecks.

Banks and Micro-finance Lending Institutions: These institutions allow their clients who meet certain requirements to apply for smaller loan amounts on agreed repayment terms.

Peer-to-Peer Lending: There are several peer-to-peer online lending sites that are open to borrowers.

Debt Settlement Agreement: This is a debt-relief option where someone negotiates with the debtor to pay less than what they owe.

Family or Friends: One can choose to borrow from friends and family. This option comes with lower interest rates to none, and the repayment period is flexible. While this isn't necessarily another business, it is an option for a consumer to not choose your services.

Credit Cards: Credit cards can be used to pay for household expenses and other bills giving the user some relief before their next paycheck.

Pawn Shops and Title Loans: These types of businesses offer loans using an item as collateral. A customer could choose to use an item of value or their car as a guarantee of repayment at one of these establishments. In the case of the pawnshop, the customer turns over ownership of the pawned item if they default on the loan. On the same terms, a title loan turns ownership of a car over to the title loan business if the customer does not repay the loan in a timely manner. These businesses can sell the item to recoup the cost of the loan. Usually, interest rates on loans with physical items as collateral are less, and the term of the loan can be a little longer than a payday advance loan, making this solution ideal for some customers who might otherwise be your customer.

Determine Income Potential

There has been a rapid growth of the payday loan business in the last few years. It is, however, a high-risk business as there are chances of lenders losing their investments as a result of loan repayment default by borrowers. Remember that some of these borrowers are people who cannot access credit from banks due to factors such as bad credit ratings. To minimize the risk of suffering losses, as a lender, you must do thorough background checks on the people you loan money to, and conduct follow-up when repayment is delayed.

Your income potential depends on how many people you are able to lend money to, what interest rate you charge, and any other associated fees you choose to enact. These rates will depend on the average expectation in your area. This is why it's important to identify your target market so you can figure out how many customers you might expect to serve. This is also why your location matters greatly.

While conducting competitor research, you should find out how much your competitors charge for their loans. You should not be the most expensive in your area, but you should also not undersell yourself. You must also consider the cost of daily running expenses and collection activities on late repayments. Finding that pricing sweet spot is key.

Interest in every $100 loan given usually varies from $15 to $25 for a 14-day loan term but higher for a month-long loan. It is very possible to make a substantial return on your investment if you efficiently run your business. This example proposes a 15-25% interest rate.

In the next chapter, you will learn about the accounting involved in running the business in regard to conducting your loans. We'll look at how to determine interest, loan fees, and profit.

Chapter 4: Understanding Financial Terms with Payday Loans

Before you can even sign on one customer, you'll need to know how to calculate interest, loan fees, and profit.

Calculating Interest

Interest paid on a payday loan is also referred to as a finance charge. It is based on the principal loan amount issued. Let's assume you issue a client with a loan worth $500 to be repaid in 14 days. You charge an interest rate of $15 for every $100 borrowed for 14 days.

Calculate your interest as follows:

>Interest = (loan amount/100)x15

>= (500/100)x15

>= 5x15

>= $75

For a loan amount of $500, your finance charge will be $75.

Understanding Loan Fees

Loan fees are charged to take care of the loan application processing expenses. It is usually 5% of the loan amount. You can use this equation to determine loan fees.

Loan fees = Loan amount x5/100

= 500x5/100

= $25

Understanding Gross Profit

The profit that you will make from a loan worth $500 in 14 days will be $75 in interest plus a $25 application fee, totaling to $100.

Let's assume that you served just 15 such clients in one week:

Total investment= $500 in loan capital x15

= $7,500

Gross profit= $100x15

= $1,500

In one week, you are able to make $1,500, considering that perhaps all of those 15 clients repay their loan on time in about 2 weeks.

Understanding Net Profit

Your net profit will be $1,500, less overhead expenses.

To maximize profits, make sure to keep your overhead expenses as low as possible. For example, you can open an online store as opposed to a physical business premises to save on the rent. Keep a close eye on employee hours, too. If your business is only supporting 15 customers a week, that's about 2 to 3 customers a day if you're open 7 days a week. You may not need more than one person to run the store every day.

Understanding APR

APR is the cost of a loan measured every year and expressed as a percentage. It includes interest and all fees charged then spread over the term of the loan. The APR is always higher than the interest rate. Reporting the APR of a loan to the consumer is required in some states.

The following information is used to calculate APR.

1. The principal loan amount

2. Finance charges

3. The loan fees

4. The loan repayment term

Using the example above:

The principal loan amount is $500, with a finance charge of $75 and loan fees of $25. The loan repayment term, usually 14 days

First, add the finance charge and the loan fee together (75+25) to get your return on investment ($100).

Second, divide the answer above by the loan principal. ($100/$500= 0.2) The figure 0.2 means you are making 20 cents for every dollar you lend out.

Then, multiply your answer above by 365 for the number of days in a year (0.2x365 = 73).

Finally, divide your answer with the loan term of 14 days (73/14= 5.214). That answer should be expressed as a percentage, so multiply it by 100. (5.214 x 100 =521.4%)

Should your client default for an entire year, you would make over 5 times the principal amount that you lent out. This is possible as most borrowers usually rollover or re-borrow the loan amount when they cannot pay off the loan all at once.

The payday loan business is very lucrative, and you can make a significant profit from it. However, exercise care by putting in place a strict loan policy. Go for clients with solid financial stability, reliable flow of income, or undisrupted flow of money.

Payday loan borrowers often have poor credit ratings, and therefore, don't qualify for bank loans. Most payday lenders charge high-interest fees as they know these people have no alternative but to borrow from them. I would advise against this approach, instead, focus on being a volume-based loan provider. Instead of maximizing profits on each loan, set goals that are unit-based because the more loans you close, the more profits you will make, and the more customers you will attract.

The payday loan business is very lucrative, and you can make a significant profit from it. However, exercise caution by putting in place a strict loan policy. Go for clients with solid financial stability, a reliable source of income, or an undisrupted flow of money.

Chapter 5: Business Investment Requirements

In this chapter, we'll discuss what you will need financially to start a payday loan business.

Start-up Costs

Adequate financial preparation is key to a successful payday loan business. Outline your initial requirements and calculate your startup costs before launching your business. When you know where you stand financially, then you can determine the following:

1. Estimate the amount of capital you require

2. Prepare a projected break-even analysis

3. Project profits in an achievable timeline

4. Attract investors

This section is an outline of the business startup costs that you should consider. Keep in mind that you have to plan ahead for recurring expenses like office rent, utilities, and salaries. Any extra cash that you have at the startup should be able to cover at least three months' worth of your operational expenses to cushion you before you turn a profit or break-even.

Here is a list of startup expenses.

Office Furniture and Equipment

Office furniture and equipment such as computers, printers, filing cabinets, chairs, desks, and phones are immediate needs. Costs range from $30,000 to $65,000 and vary according to the size of your business.

Business Registration Fees

You will need to register your business with the state either as a sole proprietorship, partnership, or limited liability. The cost of doing so ranges from $400 to $1,000.

Licenses and Permits

Licenses and permits to run the payday loan business legally will cost you between $300 and $1,000. This is a one-off annual payment.

Rent and Deposits

Rent is a recurring fixed cost ranging between $2,000 and $3,500. Rent varies greatly, depending on your chosen location. You can, however, choose to mitigate this cost by working from home, co-sharing office space, or operate the business online. Additionally, most landlords will require you to pay rent and deposit, which can be a quarterly or biannual figure.

Marketing and Advertising

We will discuss much more about marketing and advertising later, but for now, you should consider the initial cost of this very much necessary expense. If you don't advertise, no one will know you're there; hence, you won't have any customers!

Marketing and advertising will help you create awareness about your business and increase visibility to your target clients. You can do this through many different means, including flyers, signs, banners, business cards, billboards, online videos, social media, Google ads, and giveaways.

Your costs could range between $300 and $1,500 depending on the methods you choose to apply.

Website Development and Hosting

Think of getting a professional-looking, user-friendly website with easy-to-navigate pages. If you are not tech-savvy, engage a professional web designer whose fee could be between $200 and $500.

Website hosting, on the other hand, costs between $35 and $55 every month.

Office Supplies and Utilities

Your budget for office supplies such as pens, printing papers, printer ink, drinking water, and utilities might cost you $800 to $1,200 monthly.

Payroll

All of your employees will be on payroll from the onset, earning salaries, commissions, and possibly overtime, whether you make money or not. Before operating and employing anyone, plan to meet these costs out of your pocket for the first few months until your business picks up. You will also have to consider payroll taxes, usually paid quarterly, depending on your state.

Professional Consultants (such as a lawyer or accountant)

The services of an accountant will come in handy to advise you on the tax laws governing the operations of your payday loan business. The financial expert can walk you through the process of maintaining proper books of accounts, tax declaration, and offer other financial guidance and advice.

Consult a professional business lawyer to help you seal loopholes in the contracts and avoid making costly legal mistakes that rogue defaulters can exploit. The lawyer will also help you work on the legal requirements of starting and running a payday loan business.

Engage both the lawyer and the accountant on a need basis. Payday businesses spend between $1,000 and $2,500 yearly on such administration tasks.

Learn to maintain basic bookkeeping transactions for your business and reserve paid consultation for the complicated projects.

Insurance

Your business needs protection from loan defaulters, possible lawsuits, and insurable unforeseen risks. Insurance costs can be anywhere from $800 to $1,600 per year or more. Contact a business insurance company you can trust so you can get the right coverage for your business needs.

Star-up Cash for Lending

Project your loan volume and ensure you have enough liquid cash to cover the first three months. Let's assume the average amount you would be lending to be $500 to about 15 to 25 people monthly in the initial months. You will, therefore, need to have between $22,500 to $37,500 as startup lending money for the first three months. It is recommended that you plow back your profits into the business for at least 6 months until you are financially stable to start drawing out profits.

The First Three Months

Here is a table to help you gauge what your first 3 months expenses might be:

1. Rent Deposit (rent*2): 4,000 ($2,000/month rent = $6,000 for 3 months = $10,000

2. Furniture and Equipment: 30,000

3. Registration and Fees: $1,000

4. Licenses and Permits: $1,000

5. Marketing and Advertising: $1,500 first month, $500 next two months = $2,500

6. Website Development: $500 initial set up, $50/month hosting = $600

7. Professional Consultants: $3,000

8. Insurance: $1,800 ($600/month premiums)

9. Startup Cash for Lending: $7,500 to $12,500 per month = $22,500 to $37,500

12. Supplies and Utilities: $800/month = $2,400

Total: On the high end, this equals $89,800.

You could round that up to about $30,000 per month. This sounds like a high amount, but your biggest expense of this list is your cash available to lend. We also have not considered payroll expenses, so you may want to try to run the business yourself or with the help of family who are willing to donate their time at first. After three months, you may want to consider hiring help.

Finding Start-up Funds

From the table above, you will need an average of $80,000 to $90,000 to start your payday business. Access to startup capital is one of the challenges that entrepreneurs in this line of the business face. Listed below are some financing options that you can consider as a source of funding for your payday loan business. You can get funds from one or a combination of sources.

Personal Financing

Consider yourself a financier. Get capital from either your savings or collateral on your assets if you can afford it. Investing your own money puts you in full control of your business and the freedom to operate as you deem best. You are answerable to no one but yourself. The downside of personal financing is that in the case of losses, you bear the full burden yourself.

Equity Financing

You can raise capital for your payday loan business by selling a percentage of your shareholding to an interested investor. The shares issued represent a direct percentage of the amount the investor brings in, and the level of control they will have on the business. What motivates the investor to pump money into your business is the business potential.

Equity financing means you are not the sole decision-maker for most decisions concerning the business.

The advantages of equity financing include:

1. You avoid the risk of loan repayment from financing. This is helpful in the initial months of

business where possible setup costs overrun budgets.

2. The shareholder tops up your shortfall and brings in a fresh perspective different from yours.

3. Equity investors are genuinely interested in the business and will work towards its long-term success.

The disadvantages of equity financing include:

1. You and your partner share business profits in line with the shareholding percentage.

2. Shareholding takes total control and decision-making away from you.

3. The different perspectives from both of you might be a source of conflict or disagreement in the decision-making process.

Debt Financing

Debt financing involves obtaining capital funds by incurring debt at a fixed and predetermined interest rate and period. You have to repay the principal and interest by the fixed date or as per the conditions stipulated in the contract agreement.

Debt financing takes the following forms:

Friends and Family: Borrowing from family or friends can guarantee you funding with no interest and a flexible repayment period and terms. Often you require no legal documentation, but you should keep everything professional.

Angels Investors: Angels are wealthy individuals willing to invest in a business owned by other people. In the case of the payday loan business, angels bring in not just the funds, but industry knowledge, experience, and network of contacts. Most angels keep a low profile or maintain a private but active involvement in the business based on your agreement.

Bank Loans: This is a common source of funding for most startups, so long as you can convince the bank that your payday loan business is a profitable idea. Get a solid business plan and a personal guarantor.

Debt financing also carries with it several advantages:

1. Unlike equity financing, you maintain full control of your business. The lender has no say on how you run your business, and your relationship with them ends the moment you repay the debt in full.

2. The loan principal, interest, and the repayment term are agreed upon in advance. You are, therefore, able to budget and plan well.

Some disadvantages of debt financing are:

1. To qualify for debt lending, you must have an acceptable credit rating.

2. Making loan repayments may be a challenge when you develop cash flow problems.

3. Lenders will often require you to mention a personal guarantor for the business loan, and they may also attach certain business assets as collateral.

Weigh your financing options carefully and go with the most favorable one.

Chapter 6: Researching the Right Commercial Locations

The right location for your payday loan business is vital to its success and chance of survival. Unless you intend to run your business from home or online, you need to secure the right location.

Some of the places you can use to help you find a good and secure location for your payday loan business are:

- The local chamber of commerce or local councils
- Commercial real estate agencies
- Online real estate listings
- Sale or rental signs

Consider the following factors when searching for an appropriate location for your business:

Demographics

Research and gather the demographic information of the location you are interested in. Consider the population of the area, their age, and income to figure out if it fits the demographic profile of the right target market for a payday loan business. A significant percentage of that population should have a stable source of income to provide a healthy and profitable environment for your business.

Security

Your safety and that of your customers should form part of your decision-making when choosing a location for your business. Investigate the common crimes, the crime rates, and how they will possibly affect your business. Understanding the risks of potential criminal activities will influence your choice of a business location. You can choose to totally get away from that area or prepare and take additional and adequate security measures that will keep your premises safe.

Accessibility

Your payday loan business will depend on customer footfall. It is, therefore, important to ensure that your location will be easily accessible to your customers, employees, and even yourself. In case your business will be away from the main shopping area, figure out whether it will be easy for your customers to locate you or get into your premise. You also need to find out if there will be enough convenient, well maintained, and adequately lighted parking space.

Cost of Rent and Utilities

Consider your startup budget and how much you can afford to spend on rent when researching a location for your payday loan business. Take into consideration other costs apart from the monthly rent or lease, such as rent deposit, property tax, monthly utilities, and whether you will need to do renovations and improvements to the premises.

Competition

Your proximity to other competing businesses can influence the success of your business. It can either be beneficial or cause a hindrance to your growth. Nearby competitors could signal the need and presence of payday loan customers. You could benefit from customer overflow. Too much competition will make your marketing tougher and is a warning sign that you should look elsewhere as there might not be enough customers for your business. On the other hand, lack of competition shows you will have all clients to yourself but could also mean there is a lack of need for your services.

Potential for Growth

Research the location's flexibility and whether it will be able to accommodate your business growth. A small office space might be cheaper in the beginning but might limit you in the future. If you look forward to prosperity and an increase in demand for your payday loans, then you will have more customers walking into the store. More space will be needed to accommodate the increasing number of customers and the people you will employ to help in service delivery. Is the premises just a short-term location, or will it be able to serve you for the long haul?

Other Nearby Businesses

Foot traffic is important for a payday loan business, and your location in a high foot traffic area will be beneficial. Locating your shop in an area without other businesses nearby will mean you have to do more marketing and advertising to attract customers. Find out what other businesses are located in your area of interest, the customer traffic they generate, whether they serve customers who might visit your business and the possibility that their employees could become your customers.

The location you choose for your business will either set you up for success or failure. Renting or buying a storefront is quite costly and eats into a big portion of your startup investment. It is not something you can easily change. Therefore, it is important that you carry out proper research before establishing your business.

Chapter 7: Create a Business Plan

A business plan is a document prepared by an entrepreneur describing the goals of the business and the marketing, financial, and operational plans it will use to achieve the goals.

Before you start your payday loan business, you need to outline your goals and clearly state how you will achieve the said goals. Creating a business plan will help you figure this out and put in place strategies for your operations.

A good business plan should be short and precise as it is a tool that you will continuously refer to when running your business. It should also be in a language that is easy to understand. Most banks and potential investors will need to see it to decide whether your business is a worthwhile venture to invest their money. Therefore, keep your explanations simple and clear and avoid jargon and acronyms that may not be familiar to everyone.

Benefits of a Business Plan

A well-written business plan helps you get a broader picture of the whole business, and you can refer to it to adjust your strategies, as necessary. Planning helps you set priorities and strategically allocate time, energy, and resources. It acts as a constant reminder for what you should focus on for the success of the business. The plan acts as a tool for regular review of accomplishments, milestones achieved, and even setbacks and limitations. Ultimately, it helps you with financial planning.

The business plan is a roadmap of your business. While it should be written at the start of your business, it should regularly be updated. Business is always changing, and the details of your plan will change, too.

Types of Business Plans

There are two types of business plans that you can consider depending on the structure and approach of your business.

Lean Startup Business Plan

A lean business plan is meant for internal use and focuses mainly on business strategies, forecasts, and budgets. It includes financial information but not in as much detail as may be required by banks and investors. This type of business plan is mostly created by sole proprietorships who don't need funding from outside sources.

Traditional/External Business Plan

An external business plan is the most common type of business plan and is designed for external use. It provides information about the business to outsiders and is usually used by entrepreneurs to source for funding. Create a traditional business plan to showcase to potential investors how their funds will be used, what they can expect as a return on their investment, and the team that will help grow the business.

Components of a Typical Business Plan

A typical business plan is made up of the following parts. Include them when creating one for your payday loan business.

Executive Summary

The executive summary is the first thing on your business plan, but it is often written last. Introduce and explain your business concept and its benefits. It would help if you kept this section short and intriguing enough to keep the reader hooked and continue reading to the next parts for more details. Include the following information in your executive summary.

Business Concept: Describe the service that your payday loan business offers, your target market, and the competitive advantage you have over other similar companies.

Financial Plans: Clearly indicate the initial capital required and a breakdown of how the money will be spent. Include vital financial statistics, such as projected sales, balance sheet, and cash flows.

The Business Structure: Define your business structure and ownership. Is it a sole proprietorship, partnership, or a corporation, and who are the shareholders?

Company Description

This is the part where you describe your business and what it is all about. Write about the following:

a) The business structures

b) The target markets

c) The service you will provide

d) Competitors

The company description outlines information such as the service you are offering, the objectives, vision, and location of your company.

Begin this section with a short description of the general money lending industry. The industry's present outlook, markets available, other related services or developments that could benefit your business or potentially pose a risk to it, and the growth experienced. Be sure to base this information on reliable and relevant sources. Do not make assumptions. It could land you in trouble when seeking funding.

When describing your business, include the following elements:

Company Name: This is the registered official name of the business.

Business Structure: Describe your method of operation. Is it store-based or online-based? State whether the business is a startup or an acquisition. Describe the company's legal structure, whether it is a sole proprietorship, partnership, or corporation. Discuss the principle owners, their equity share and responsibilities in the business

Ownership: Provide the names of the business principle owners, their equity shares, and duties to the company. Include the names and roles of any other key personnel.

Objectives: Outline your business goals and the achievements you would like to accomplish within a given time frame.

Location: Describe the location of your business and its accessibility.

Company History: State when the business was started and the inspiration behind it.

Company's Mission Statement: Make a clear statement that reflects the goals and values that your business stands for.

Company's Vision Statement: Make a statement on the business's current and future objectives.

The Product: Give a clear description of what you are offering and the need that it fulfills. Emphasize its unique features from what is already provided by others in the industry. Talk about your target market and the strategies you will employ to reach them, e.g., advertising and promotions.

Competitive Edge: Describe how your business will achieve a competitive advantage and what makes your product better than what is already available in the market.

Profitability Factor: Show that your payday loan business will be profitable by explaining those factors that will propel it to success, for example, the presence of a ready market. If you intend to seek funding, an investor will want to know if the business will be profitable enough to give them a return on their investment. Explain why you need the extra funding and how it is going to impact on the business profitability.

Tips for writing a good company description include:

- Prepare and organize all the vital information to include in the company description.

- Make your introductory paragraph appealing and captivating. Include vital information that will capture the attention of the reader and stay hooked.

- Information and explanations that are captured in other sections of the business plan to be made short and precise.

- When explaining why you started the business, your tone should show excitement and passion.

- Make your sentences clear and to the point and avoid repeating yourself or being wordy.

- Ask someone knowledgeable to proofread the draft for any typos, grammatical mistakes, and any other errors.

The Overall Business Opportunity

Provide the following information in this section:

The services you will provide: Describe the problems that face your target market and how the payday loans will benefit them.

Your target market: Describe your target market. Understanding who you will provide your loan services to will help you build your marketing strategy and plan your growth.

Identify your market trends: Describe relevant notable trends and how these trends will favor your business.

Describe your expected market growth: Explain the growth experienced in the industry as a whole and strategies you will implement for your business to gain from it.

Competition: Describe who your competitors are and what differentiates you and the competitive advantage you have over them.

Marketing Plan

A marketing plan is a document that describes the strategies you intend to use to use to reach out to your target audience. You need to persuade and convince people to borrow loans from you. A well-developed marketing plan that is backed by factual data will help you clearly define your marketing strategies.

A practical and results-oriented marketing plan is made up of the following elements:

Market Analysis

The first step to creating an effective marketing plan for your business is to analyze your strengths, weakness, opportunities, and threats. This is called a SWOT analysis.

Strengths are the factors that give you a competitive edge over your competitors. It could be that you have a larger capital base than them, and you are capable of lending more. Identify these strengths and plan to make full use of them.

Weaknesses are the inside factors that can potentially reduce your ability to succeed, such as inadequate marketing skills.

Opportunities are favorable external factors, chances, or openings that your business could exploit for growth. An example is expanding to new markets.

Threats are outside factors that could hurt your business, such as changes in government regulations regarding payday loan businesses.

Additionally, find out who your competitors are. Understand the strengths they have over you, weaknesses that you can use to your advantage, and how they generally run their business.

Market analysis provides the following benefits:

1. You become acquainted with all aspects of the market, making it easy to define your target market.

2. You are in a position to make informed decisions on how to price your loans and apply marketing strategies.

3. You can understand the growth potential for your business and plan for it.

Marketing Goals

State your business mission and define specific goals and the timelines within which you wish to achieve them. The goals should be realistic and also measurable for ease of performance evaluation. For example, your marketing goal could be to increase your lending by 10% in the first quarter.

Target Market

Without customers, there is no business. To correctly structure your marketing strategy, you need to understand your potential customers. The following insights will help you structure your loans better and outshine your competitors.

- Profile your target market based on demographics such as age, gender, geographic location, employment status, income level, and spending habits. Profiling helps you determine their needs.

- Estimate demand for payday loans as well as the estimated growth rate. When you can establish adequate demand, you become confident about your business success, and your investors become assured of growth.

- Understand why your target market needs payday loans. Is it to take care of a financial emergency, or is their income not sufficient enough to last them through the month?

- Establish why they would borrow from you and not your competitors.

After defining the target market, break it down to determine what portion of this market is feasible. A feasible market is that part of the target market that you can acquire with the current structure and outlook of the money lending industry as a whole, competition, your marketing strategies, and available funds for lending.

Marketing Strategies

Define your marketing strategies, the marketing vehicle you intend to use to reach your target market and convert them into your borrowers. The choice of marketing strategy should be appropriate and relevant to the target audience you defined above. The marketing mix made of the 4 P's is usually combined to form a strong marketing strategy.

The 4 P's of marketing are:

Product: In our case, this is payday loans.

Price: Price here refers to the finance charge and any other fees charged on the principal loan amount. Your pricing directly impacts the success of your business as borrowers will always compare against that of your competitors. However, the basic rule is that your pricing must cover all operational costs. To price your loan better, you have to reduce your overhead expenditure. Pricing can always be adjusted to reflect market dynamics, such as demand and competitor activities.

Place: Place refers to the channels you will use to conduct your operations. Will your business operate from a storefront, or will it rely on online-based transactions or both? Your choice should be based on your target market characteristics, channels adopted by your competitors, and available company resources.

Promotion: Promotion is the channel of communication that you will use to inform your target market about your payday loan business. Promotion helps put the service in the customers' minds and persuades them to borrow from you. The choice of promotion strategy should be selected by knowing your target audience and the goal that you intend to achieve.

Some promotional strategies include traditional and online advertising. With advertising, you can reach a large number of your target audience at the same time.

Consider these advertising methods:

- Television
- Radio
- Newspapers
- Magazines
- Billboards
- Social media such as Facebook, Twitter, Instagram
- Website/Blog
- Text Messaging
- YouTube Videos

You could also consider the following:

Personal Selling: Personal selling focuses on building and cultivating long-term relationships and partnerships with potential customers. It involves reaching out to them on a one on one interaction, through a phone call or over electronic mail.

Direct Marketing: Direct marketing involves reaching a selected small audience with specifically tailored messages for them. The message can be communicated through postal mail, email, or social media platforms.

Discounts: Offer short term discounts to entice borrowers to your business. Perhaps you could consider offering waiving application fees or a lowered finance charge when they refer a friend to your business.

Referrals: Ask your clients for references from their network of friends, relatives, and colleagues. To build trust and credibility, offer them the best customer service, and ask for honest feedback. Word of mouth is a powerful advertisement channel, so be sure to keep your clients happy and satisfied.

Influencers: Influencers are people who your potential customers listen to and look up to. They could be celebrities such as radio presenters, TV personalities, YouTube channel hosts, or Instagram stars. Nurture a relationship with these people as they can help build your brand. Some influencers you could consider partnering with might be lifestyle vloggers, mommy bloggers/Instagram stars, or anyone in the world of finance. Just be sure that the influencer you choose targets your potential market.

Create ads with emotional content: Connect with your clients through emotional ads. Your clients are human and emotional. Please take advantage of this and come up with ad content that will evoke their emotions.

You will need a team with the right skills and experience to help you to develop and implement your marketing plan. Depending on the available resources, you can employ a marketing expert either on a permanent basis, contractual agreement, or get a volunteer or an intern.

Financial Plan

A financial plan will help you estimate how much capital you will require and a glimpse of how your business will fair. Use the following sales and forecasts for the first few years:

- Projected profit and loss statement
- Projected cash flow statement
- Sales forecast
- Balance sheet

A financial plan comes last in your marketing plan. It shows a breakdown of costs associated with each strategy and the operating expenses you are likely to incur. Prepare a budget and a sales forecast to establish projected expenses and income. Make revisions until you come up with a final budget that falls within your initial capital.

Prepare a break-even analysis to establish how much profit you need to make to cover your operating costs.

Chapter 8: Legal Matters

In the United States, each state has unique regulations on payday loan lending. The features of payday loans vary geographically, with each state charging different fees and applying varying penalties on unrepaid loans. Some of the features of payday loans that vary from state to state include:

- Legal status of a payday loan business. Some locales have outlawed payday loans

- Maximum amounts that can be borrowed at any given time

- Interest rates caps, finance charge, and APR limits

- Number of rollovers allowed

- Installments allowed

- Loan term limits

Lenders, therefore, choose the features of their loans depending on the regulations of the states where they operate. For example, lenders give out loan amounts that match their state regulations while there are wide variations in amounts issued in those states that do not have such rules. The average loan interest charged in states that regulate interest rates is $17 for $100 principal amount, while states that haven't capped interest rates are $24 per $100 loan.

States are categorized into three groups, each depending on the type of payday loan regulations that they adopt.

Restrictive States

These are states that have very strict rules that prohibit lending of payday loans, or the usury laws are so restrictive that such businesses can no longer take place. In states that prohibit payday loan businesses, there are no storefront or online lenders.

Arizona	Arkansas	Washington, DC
Maryland	Massachusetts	New Jersey
New York	North Carolina	Vermont
West Virginia	Connecticut	Georgia
Montana	New Hampshire	Pennsylvania

Hybrid States

To operate in these states, payday loan lenders are required to adhere to the following rules.

- Cap their interest rates with APRs allowed to reach 3-digit numbers.
- The number of loans offered to a borrower is restricted.
- Borrowers to be allowed multiple repayment periods.

The following states practice hybrid payday lending:

Colorado	Florida	Maine
Oregon	Virginia	Washington
Minnesota	Rhode Island	

Permissive States

In these states, lenders are at liberty to operate. The lenders here charge interest rates from 15% with very high APRs. These states are:

| Alaska | Alabama | California | Delaware | Hawaii |

Idaho	Illinois	Indiana	Ohio	Kansas
Kentucky	Louisiana	Michigan	Mississippi	Missouri
Nebraska	Nevada	New Mexico	North Dakota	Oklahoma
Utah	South Carolina	South Dakota	Tennessee	Texas

Federal Guidelines and Regulations

Some of the legislative regulations that have taken place in the payday loan industry over the years include:

Usury Laws and Usury Caps

Usury is a Latin word that means lending money at high-interest rates. In the United States, laws touching on usury were introduced in 1965 and have been updated and restricted over the years. Usury laws restrict the interest rates that lenders charge. Today, several states have placed usury caps on payday loans ranging from 6% to 36%. Lenders are obliged to adhere to such interest rate caps.

States have either taken restrictive or prohibitive actions to bring order and fairness to the payday loan industry. Fourteen states and the District of Columbia have capped their interest at 36%. Since 2005, there has not been a new state that has authorized high-interest rate lending.

Military Lending Act (2006)

Payday loans offered to service members were capped at 36% APR from October 2007. Charges are also included in the rate. The Act requires that military borrowers must be given disclosures on the loan costs. Lenders usually require that such customers sign a statement showing their military association.

States Take Action to Stop Payday Lenders Exploitation (2008)

States like North Carolina, Arkansas, Arizona, Washington DC, Montana, New Hampshire, Ohio, Oregon, Colorado, and Virginia have put in place regulations to reduce consumer exploitations by payday loan lenders.

Prohibition of Bank Payday Loans (2014)

Practices by banks to offer loans whose features were similar to that of payday loans were discontinued.

Truth in Lending Act (TILA)

This Act protects the borrower from unfair loan charges. Lenders are required to make full disclosure of the loan cost. Borrowers can then use this information to compare the costs offered by other loan providers. TILA also protects borrowers from high-pressure sales strategies by lenders. Borrowers have a rescission right. They are allowed three days to reconsider their decision to borrow, and should they decide to back out of the process, the lender shall not impose any penalties on them.

Proposals by The Consumer Financial Protection Bureau (CFPB)

Consumer Financial Protection Bureau (CFPB) was created in 2010 by the US government to educate and protect its citizens on financial matters. CFPB is an independent agency whose task is to ensure that all federal laws are adhered to.

A new proposal was drawn in 2017 by the CFPB. Some states had failed to abide by the set payday loan pricing and affordability policy. The APR has skyrocketed to almost 700%. This new proposal had the following aims:

1. To increase consumer protection through an advance affordability check.

2. Limit the lender's ability to directly withdraw money from the borrower's bank account without authorization from the borrower.

The deadline for compliance with these rules was August 2019. However, these new regulations were shelved until November 2020, giving payday lenders some reprieve.

Loan Collection Policy

Legal debt collection practices in the United States include collection calls, letters, and sometimes lawsuits. Lenders are prohibited from calling a borrower's employer or issuing arrest threats. Failing to repay a loan is not considered a criminal offense as per Federal rules. Lenders, therefore, cannot initiate a criminal procedure against a borrower unless the lender can provide evidence of a non-repayment intention.

Consulting a Lawyer

Hiring and consulting a qualified lawyer is necessary to ensure that you comply with the laws set by your state to regulate payday loan businesses. You may also need a lawyer when faced with a legal situation or need help with specific legal issues. Legal assistance is essential to the success of your business. With the right legal guidance, you will be able to save a lot of money and build an excellent reputation for your business.

Why You Need a Lawyer

1. To help you understand the legal and regulatory requirements involved in starting and running a payday business such as acquiring the right licenses and to enact the correct loan features.

2. To provide guidance when writing contracts. Contracts involve negotiations and document preparations that you may not be familiar with. You may hire a lawyer to oversee this process and ensure that the contract is valid.

3. To review legally binding agreements to protect you from bad contracts that may have detrimental legal consequences.

4. To help handle legal issues that may arise in your business, such as lawsuits from customers or employees. The lawyer will help protect your legal rights as well as your business interests.

5. To help you with debt recovery and management. A lawyer will advise on the best ways to handle borrowers who refuse to repay a loan and the legalities involved. Non-repayment or late repayments can stifle your ability to grow your business

6. To guide you in choosing the right insurance coverage. The insurance coverage you purchase should ensure that you comply with the relevant regulations and protect it from personal liability should the business run into problems in the future.

Your business may not always need a lawyer as you can handle some matters on your own. However, you are advised to seek the help of a qualified lawyer for complicated or time-consuming issues.

What to Look for When Hiring a Lawyer

When hiring a lawyer, be sure to get one who:

- Can quickly understand the legal needs of your business.
- Ability to prepare the right contracts for your borrowers and business partners.
- Can review the contracts that others (like the landlord) will bring for signing.

When interviewing potential lawyers, find out the following:

1. **Level of experience**: Find out if they have previously handled business with similar legal needs as yours. For example, do they understand the federal laws that you need to comply with?

2. **Connection**: Most lawyers have a specialty, and the one you are interviewing will probably not know

everything about all areas of law. However, they should know or have a working relationship with other lawyers who can step in for them whenever the need arises.

3. **Whether they are representing a competitor:** A lawyer with experience in payday loan businesses is great. It should be a concern, though, if they are currently representing one or more other payday lenders who are your direct competitors. The lawyer could accidentally or intentionally leak your sensitive and confidential information to your competitors. A legal code of ethics bounds lawyers, but you shouldn't take such a risk.

4. **Communication and teaching skills**: A lawyer will need to explain the legal requirements, how they are likely to affect your operations, and how to spot them early enough for prompt action. The right lawyer should be one who can communicate effectively and be ready to take their time to teach you and your partners or employees.

How to Save on Legal Bills

Lawyers can be expensive, and it is recommended that you do on your own the tasks that are within your capability. Consult a lawyer only on complex or matters that can take up so much of your time. Hire your lawyer on a contract basis and adopt a billing system that is convenient for you. Below are some of the ways that lawyers bill their clients:

a) **Hourly billing**: Your lawyer will most probably bill by the hour. Make sure to specify the hourly rate on your contract.

b) **Flat fee**: Some lawyers prefer a flat rate fee for the task they will perform.

c) **Monthly retainer**: You and your lawyer can agree on a specific amount to pay monthly for all legal services

d) **Contingent fee**: This is a fee that you pay your lawyer should they succeed in recovering payment. Often time the fee is anywhere between 25% to 40%

of the recovered amount. Should they fail, they are only entitled to recover their out of pocket expenses. Specify in advance the expenses that you will reimburse.

Chapter 9: Employee Matters

You may be able to handle your business operations by yourself at the beginning. However, as the business grows, you will need some helping hands to remain competitive and successful.

Having competent, hardworking, and loyal employees in the right positions will help you build a successful and reputable payday loan business. The number of posts to fill, the qualifications of candidates, and the salaries to pay, should be informed by your business goals, vision, and affordability.

Hiring the right employees is crucial to building a prosperous payday loan company. When hiring, look for candidates who show commitment and loyalty. Inquire about their past employment and durations they stayed in those companies. Hiring a candidate who switches jobs frequently will not be suitable for your business.

Hire employees with the right skills, educational background, and experience needed for the particular position you are looking to fill. However, do not just hire based on their resume and the confidence they exude during the interview. Test their learning and analytical skills, as well.

Before you bring a new employee on board, check their compatibility with your business culture. Find out if they are customer-centric and if they will get along with the other employees. Inquire about their relationship with the current employer, colleagues, and clients. You can then make your judgment.

Consider creating and filling the following positions within your payday loan business for efficient and profitable operations.

Chief Executive Officer

- Provide leadership and ensures effectiveness in the operations of the company by recruiting, training, disciplining, assigning roles, and appraising.

- Ensure the implementation of the company's vision, mission, and overall business strategies.

- Responsible for fixing and reviewing loan interest rates and fees

- Signs checks and documents on behalf of the business

- Responsible for the overall success of the organization

Loan Consultants

- Responsible for payday loan applications, processing, and administration

- Responsible for recording and filing borrowers' details

- Provide financial advice to borrowers

- Accountable for client follow-ups to ensure the loan is paid back.

Administrative/Human Resource Manager

- Ensure the smooth running of administrative and human resource related duties

- Ensure the availability of office supplies and that any office repairs and maintenance required are carried out

- Responsible for successful interviewing and recruitment process

- Carry out employee indoctrination to new recruits

- Carry out evaluation and assessment of employees

- Arrange for travel and schedules meetings and appointments

Marketing and Sales Executive

- Identify and reach out to potential payday loan borrowers

- Follow up on leads and contacts both physically and electronically

- Participate in the structuring of marketing strategies and ensures that marketing plans are carried out to completion

- Carry out market surveys and feasibility studies

- Responsible for documenting all customer information

Accountant

- Prepare financial reports, budgets, and financial statements for the organization

- Record and create reports on all financial transactions

- Prepare the income statement and balance sheet for the company

- Provide financial and risk analyses, budgets, and all accounting reports

- Analyze financial feasibility for proposed projects such as marketing plans and carry out financial forecasting

- Manage and develop financial systems and policies

- Responsible for administration of employee payrolls and ensure compliance with taxation laws

- Act as the company's internal financial auditor

Customer Care Representative

- Warmly receive visitors and customers

- Respond to business phone calls and direct inquiries to the right respondent

- Provide personalized and professional customer care services to clients

- Use their interaction with clients be it on phone, email, or text to build relationships with them and create interest

- Provide helpful and accurate information to customers

Company Handbook

I would strongly suggest that you create a company-wide handbook of rules, regulations, business directives, and job descriptions that all employees can access, so they are on the same page. I would suggest making this required reading for any new hire. Some topics to include in your company handbook are:

- Company mission statement

- Safety and emergency policies and regulations

- Sick policy

- Attendance policy

- Dress code expectations

- Delegation of tasks by job

- Store operation hours

- Who to call in emergencies, break-ins, robberies, etc.

- Money handling procedures

- Facilities maintenance procedures

- Job review process/how to get raise or promotions

- Discipline procedures for misconduct including what actions result in immediate termination vs. a warning or write-up

- Grievance procedures/suggestion submissions

Chapter 10: More About Marketing and Advertising

For your payday loan business to thrive, you need to be able to attract and retain borrowers. Marketing your business will help create awareness for your payday loans, capture the attention of the audience, generate leads, and persuade potential borrowers.

Most people who take out payday loans do so to meet short-term financial pitfalls and urgent financial obligations. Your marketing message should, therefore, communicate and emphasize that your business can help the borrower meet such financial obligations. Your marketing message and language should also emphasize on your business commitment to client privacy. Most payday loan borrowers would like their transactions to be kept discreet.

Payday loan borrowers usually need money almost immediately. Make the loan application process simple and fast. Give your customers the option to send their applications online. You, therefore, need to create your payday loan business website. Additionally, many people use the internet to search for information about payday loans. Your website should provide relevant information to capture potential borrower's attention.

A professional website is an essential part of a business. If you intend to carry out digital advertising campaigns as a marketing strategy for your business, then you will need a professional company website for such campaigns to be successful. Digital advertising campaigns are designed to drive traffic to a website.

A useful website should be carefully designed to attract, capture visitors' attention, and persuade them to take out your loans. Such a website will also help build trust with the customers.

How to Create Your Payday Loan Business Website

Creating a website is a simple process. Here are the steps to follow:

Register Your Domain Name

Your domain name is the website name and address that will be used to find your business. It is recommended that you choose a domain name that matches your company name for a professional look. We have discussed business names and domain names at length previously.

Get a Website Host

A website host will host and store your website content in an always up and running a secure server. Without web hosting, your website will not be visible or accessible. The domain provider can also be the host unless you prefer otherwise.

Design Your Website and Create Content

Design, customize, and add branding elements to the website. Then create essential website pages and fill them with relevant information. These pages include;

1. **Homepage**: This is the first page that visitors come to when they click on your website.

2. **About page**: The page that explains what the website and your payday loans are about

3. **Contact page**: The page where you list the contact details through which interested clients can reach you.

4. **Blog page**: The page where you list all your payday loan business-related blog posts or company news and announcements.

5. **Loan application page**: Load your online application form here.

Your website design should be user-friendly and as simple as possible with just enough information. Too many pages, clutter, and graphics can be overwhelming and distracting to users. Your website visitors may, therefore, have a hard time finding the information they need, thus taking longer to decide whether to apply for your loans or not. Include only the necessary and relevant information. Use simple and sleek designs that will allow users to quickly navigate and find the information they need for decision making.

Use pictures and visual cues instead of block texts to lead your website users to sections you would want them to go. For example, you can use pictures to point toward a lead box or arrows towards a conversion point, such as a loan application form.

Remember to use pictures with high resolution. The pictures should also match the style of your website. Instead of texts, use infographics as most website users just skim through the website instead of reading in detail.

Incorporate aesthetic elements such as pleasing color pallets, typography, and balance to make your website visually appealing to the users. A visually appealing website has a high chance of catching the attention of a user and even convert them into a borrower.

Your website layout should be easy for visitors to navigate. Stick to designs that users are familiar with and find easy to use. Such a layout should have at the top of each page; a navigation menu, a search bar to the right-hand side, and a clickable logo to take the user back to the home page. The bottom of each page includes your business contact details. Links to a website should have a different font color.

Have a consistent layout, matching color scheme, fonts, and image style across all the website pages.

Consistency throughout the website design can help build trust with your users.

Make the information flow pattern logical, organized, and easy to follow. Essential information about your payday loans should be at the top while the least important at the bottom of the web page. Display your important conversion points such as 'Apply now' above the fold of each page and a large and easy to identify 'submit' button at the end of the application form.

Your website loading time should just take a few seconds. Users might abandon your website if it took longer to load. To improve on the load time, reduce the size of images and files. If this action does not make the load time any better, consider upgrading your server.

Your web design should be such that your website can be available and accessible on all operating systems (e.g., android, windows), browsers (e.g., Google Chrome, opera mini), and devices (computers, tablets, and phones).

Overall, your website design should be centered around the goals you wish to achieve through the website. The purpose of the website should be clear, upfront, and evident throughout the web design.

Search Engine Optimization (SEO)

Make your business website an excellent marketing tool by increasing its visibility to web search engine users. SEO can help your website rank high when searches come up for topics related to payday loans in search engines such as Google. SEO achieves this by incorporating keywords that can create leads to your website.

When search engine users key in your keywords, relevant pages of your website will appear as one of the top results; therefore, you must use keywords that are frequently searched by potential clients as well as those targeted by competing companies.

Launching an Affiliate Site

Another strategy you can use to reach many potential borrowers through your website is the use of affiliate marketers. Create an affiliate program to encourage other people (affiliates) to promote your payday loan business. You can also join an already existing external affiliate network.

An affiliate could either be an individual who promotes your business on social media or a website owner who promotes your business to their target market. Through these affiliates, you can market your payday loans business without doing the promotion yourself. This advertising arrangement is referred to as 'Affiliate Marketing.'

Affiliate marketing, an online sales strategy, will help you increase your lending by allowing affiliates to market your loans to their target audience. The affiliates then get a commission for every successful conversion.

Many people surf the internet daily but don't visit your website either because they don't know such a business exists or they have never been interested in payday loans. However, the internet user could be interested in some other closely related subjects such as 'How to manage my finances wisely.' If the website from where the internet user is reading is your affiliate, they could recommend payday loans for emergency financial bail-out and provide a link to your website.

Should the reader be interested, they would then click on the link to your website and apply for a loan. This one borrower could even become a repeat client or refer others to the site. You will have, therefore, made a sale without advertising while the affiliate marketer made some money without owning a payday loan business but by just incorporating yours into their website.

An affiliate marketer can link your payday loan business website using many methods. The decision on which method is best to use will depend on what is most suitable for both of you, and the goal you intend to achieve through affiliate marketing.

Text Link

A text link is the most common method used by affiliate marketers to link merchant sites. In this method, the affiliate will hyperlink your website on their site's content (hypertext). A hypertext is content with hyperlink. When a user clicks or taps on the hypertext, the browser will bring up your website. Text links are ingrained in the affiliate's web site's content and, therefore, don't look like advertisements.

Banner Links

Use banner links if you feel that text links don't help much to attract visitors from the affiliate's site to your website. Banner links are rectangular boxes with graphic elements and text promoting your payday loans business. The banner link is displayed across the top, bottom, or sides of the affiliate website. The purpose of banner links is to get traffic to your website

Search Box

A search box is a rectangular field on the affiliate's site that allows visitors to launch a search. The search box leads to other links on the website. An affiliate marketer could use the search box as a straight forward link to your website's home page or as a direct link to your payday loan application form.

Affiliate Tracking Software

Use an affiliate tracking link/software to keep track of your affiliates. The tracking software will also help you know when a visitor to the affiliate sites clicked on your website or a page that promotes your loans. The URL for affiliates contains the affiliate's identification number, your business identification number, and your website URL.

The tracking link helps you identify the affiliate marketer who helped convert a lead into an actual borrower. You are thus able to know who to compensate for a sale.

Payment Arrangement for Affiliate Marketers

Pay-per-sale

In this kind of arrangement, you pay an affiliate only when they send you a client who borrows from you. You can either pay the affiliate marketer a percentage of the interest charged or a fixed amount on the principal amount.

Pay-per-click

In this arrangement, you pay the affiliate marketer based on an agreed number of clicks on the link to your business website. For example, you could agree to pay the affiliate a certain amount of money per 100 clicks. It does not matter whether the clicks lead to a sale or not.

Pay-per-lead

Cost-per-lead is a payment arrangement where you pay the affiliate based on the number of website visitors who show interest in your payday loans and sign up as leads. You provide the affiliate with a form that, when filled by a visitor, counts as a sales lead.

How to Find Affiliates

You may think this whole affiliate marketing thing is awesome, and you, for sure, want to get in on it. But how do you find people willing to be affiliates?

Insert the Affiliate Program Link on Your Business Website

Affiliates often search through business websites for affiliate program links. Insert the link at the footer for ease of location. Give a clear and easy to understand terms, commission structures, and payment options.

Existing Clients

Your clients are the best affiliates you can have. Existing clients understand how your business operates and the benefits of payday loans. To convert them to affiliates, ensure your clients are happy and satisfied with your offers. Have a professional and active customer care service that sees to it that no client is disgruntled. You can then encourage the borrowers to make some money for themselves by referring their friends, colleagues, and family to borrow from you. These customers can help market your business through their social media platforms or just word of mouth.

Email Signature

Include your affiliate program link in your email signature so that the people you email can know about it.

Influencers

Influencers are people with a substantial public following. Influencers can mold peoples' opinions about your payday loans. Influencers can be famous personalities, such as celebrities or people with specific expertise. Build a long-term relationship with these influencers. Make them understand the benefits of your payday loans and request them to do positive public reviews.

Blogs

Most blogs provide helpful information regarding the topic of the blogger's choice. Established blogs are often quite prevalent among readers with the same interest. Offer your affiliate program to bloggers whose blog contents match or relate to your payday loans. Give them a creative approach and an offer that will be worth catching their attention. These bloggers are probably getting similar requests from other business people or are already working with other affiliates.

Affiliate Conferences

Take part in an affiliate conference whenever they are organized. Affiliates usually hold conferences to get a platform to exchange their experiences, news, knowledge, and new technologies relevant to their work. Affiliates also attend these conferences with the hope of meeting new partners. Take advantage of such opportunities to find affiliates ready to promote your payday business to their audience.

Online Marketing

There are several business promotions groups with many active members on social media. Join these groups and scout for potential affiliates. Identify the most active and influential members and talk to them about your affiliate program and how they can make money off it.

You can also advertise the affiliate program on social media to attract affiliates.

Affiliate Networks

Affiliate marketers looking for businesses to promote often check with their affiliate network sites. You can list your business with these network sites so that interested affiliates can find you. You will, however, have to pay a registration fee to list on these affiliate networks. Another alternative would be to pay a certain percentage as commission for any successful for every successful sale made.

How to Attract the Best Affiliates

- Reach out to affiliates whose website content complement or are relevant to payday loan services.

- Give clear terms like who gets a commission when a conversion is made.

- Lay down simple commission agreements and payment options.

- Offer commissions that can motivate and attract the best affiliates

- Reward your affiliates with higher commissions or performance bonuses when they do a good job.

- Show support by creating marketing materials and promotional articles that affiliates can use to make their work easier.

- Persuade potential affiliates with gifts

Advertising Strategies

As a startup business, you need to invest in advertising to create awareness about your payday loan business. It is also recommended that you regularly advertise to help you grow your client base and increase your lending.

A successful advertising campaign should largely depend on the characteristics of your target audience. There are two different advertising approaches: traditional and online advertising. Both approaches will enable you to reach a large number of your target audience at the same time.

Find out who your competitors are, where and how they advertise, and the messages their adverts carry. You can apply the same strategy as them or try out a different approach. Get creative with your advertising campaigns to increase your business visibility, but remember to stay within the regulations.

Advertising should target the appropriate audience.

Advertising your payday loan business will cost you some money. Your advertising campaign should, therefore, reach your target market to maximize your budget and get value for your money. In your business plan, you identified your potential clients and profiled them. Use that information to choose an advertising channel that suits them.

Consider your target audience location and ensure that your advertising will reach them. Billboards, for example, should be placed where there is high traffic such that your audience is most likely to see them.

Advertising should be timed well.

Plan your adverts to run during the time of the day that you are sure to catch the attention of your target audience. For example, if you choose television as your medium, plan to have your adverts run when most people are watching such as during primetime or in the evenings and early hours of the night when people are home and most likely watching TV.

Once your business is established, it would be best to run your ads during the peak or most productive times of the year. Study your customers borrowing patterns and plan your advertising campaigns wisely. If people borrow more when schools are about to open, then, advertising around this time will help increase your lending.

Campaigns should be measurable and trackable.

Evaluate performance and compare the success of your advertisements to help you make informed decisions on your future campaigns. You must understand whether the campaigns yielded the desired results or not. If not, then you will need to go back to the drawing board and find out where the advertising went wrong or use a different channel altogether.

Advertising Channels

Television

Television is a powerful advertising channel as it has an extensive reach. Many people spend their free time watching something on TV. You are, therefore, able to reach a wider audience and communicate to them about your payday loan business and its benefits. With expertly produced ads and a good script, you will be able to quickly grab the attention of the viewer when the ad is run.

One of the reasons why TV ads are effective is that TV combines sight, sound, and color, therefore, grabbing the attention of viewers and drawing them to the ad. You can create a script that fosters emotions that your target audience can relate with when they see and hear.

For an effective television advertising campaign, plan to run your ads at a time that you are sure of reaching a majority of your audience. Payday loans generally target those with a source of income, such as a job. These people will always be away from the house during the day. You can, therefore, buy evening TV advertising spots when the audience is most likely back to the house and relaxed.

However, advertising on television can be very costly. First, you need to produce quality ads, which don't come cheap. Inferior ads can be disastrous as they can dent the reputation of your business, thereby losing borrowers to competitors.

Second, television advertising is sold in units measured in seconds. The cost of these slots varies with the time of running the advert and the television channel of use. For your advert to stick in the minds of your audience, you need to run your advert several times in a day, which pushes your costs even higher.

You may need to make a change to your television ad. Either because of a mistake in the ad or a change you have implemented in your business offer that you need to communicate to your audience. Changing a TV ad is not easy or cheap. It will cost you some money to re-shoot the whole ad or re-shoot the part that needs changing. It can also be challenging to get the initial feeling that the ad had.

Radio

Radio is another advertising channel that you can use to reach your target audience and persuade them to borrow your loans. Radio offers you the chance to communicate with a targeted group of potential borrowers. Radio advertising is usually cheaper as compared to TV advertising.

Radio stations practice selective targeting where a station targets a specific demographic. You can, therefore, choose to advertise your payday loans on a radio station that best fits your market segment. You can go further and use a popular radio presenter to deliver your radio ad when they are on air, thus boosting your advertising campaign.

Radio advertisements are memorable as sound can be stored in memory for longer durations. Ensure you create a memorable jingle for a compelling radio advertising campaign.

With radio advertising, you require minimal effort and financing. You can write and produce an ad copy yourself or pay an advertising agency to come up with one. Your ad copy should be catchy, simple, easy to understand. The ad message should also include a call to action. Furthermore, it should give the audience your location, business website, and company phone number. Remember to repeat the important points in the ad message several times.

To advertise on the radio, you will need to buy spots, which could be 15, 30, or 60 seconds long. The cost of these spots will depend on the frequency with which you would like your ad to be played. Cost is another factor that will determine the cost of radio advert is the time of day of the ad broadcast. Running your ads during the morning (6 a.m. to 10 a.m.) or evening (3 p.m. to 7 p.m.) shows will cost you more as this is the time that radio listenership peaks. Radio cost will also depend on whether you need actors to read your script.

Advertising on the radio also poses some challenges. Most radio listeners do not pay close attention to what is said. Listeners are always disrupted by one thing or the other. Those driving maybe too focused on the road and don't pay attention to the adverts.

Lack of visual appeal makes it difficult for listeners to remember what they heard. You, therefore, have to run your ad regularly to create an impact. Without this, you may not realize any significant results from the radio ad.

Newspaper

Advertising in your local or national newspaper is another way to reach a large number of your target audience. Newspaper ads are effective, mainly when they target older people as they tend to read newspapers more. Although a large group of people reads newspapers, you can still target your ads right. Request the newspapers to run your payday loan business ad in the pages that your target audience would be more interested in, such sections as business, sports, or politics.

Newspaper advertising costs vary depending on the size of the ad, section of ad placement, the ad frequency, and type.

Newspapers, however, have the disadvantage of limited readership. Quite a large number of people may not see or read your ad. Another limitation related to this channel of advertising is that you only get to know the general section where your ad will be placed. As an advertiser, you don't get to decide exactly where the ad is displayed.

Magazines

Magazines are niche publications that cater to a specific audience. You, therefore, have the option to choose a magazine that precisely targets people with the potential to be your borrowers. Some magazines are also meant for specific regions or geographical areas. You can choose to advertise through such magazines to reach only people within your locality. It is cheaper to advertise in local/regional magazines than the national ones.

Magazines have a longer shelf life as compared to newspapers. As newspapers become stale by the end of the day, newspapers can be kept and read over a more extended period. Your ad will, therefore, be able to reach your audience long after it was placed.

Magazine advertising is, however, usually more expensive compared to newspaper advertising. Magazines also attract a narrow segment of interested readers, thus limiting your advertising audience reach. Magazines are also known to take a significant amount of time between publications.

Some are published weekly, while a majority are monthly publications. You, therefore, have to wait longer after developing your brand message to start getting leads. Competing ads on the magazine may also cause clutter making it hard for your ad to stand out.

You may want to target locally-produced magazines and publications. Many localities have a community-focused magazine, which is often free for the consumer to read. This would be a publication like an "Auto Trader" type magazine, which thrives on used car sales ads. This would reach a very local audience.

Billboards

Billboards are large-scale print advertisements. This is another effective way for you to raise awareness for your payday loans business. When placed in high traffic or busy areas, billboard ads can broadcast your message to a large number of people, including drivers and pedestrians, throughout the day. Most people use the same routes every day to work and back home. Seeing a billboard over and over sticks the message in the customer's memory.

Unlike newspapers, you have full control of where a billboard advertisement is to be placed. It is recommended that you position your billboard ad along roads and highways where prospective borrowers drive or walk by frequently. A strategic billboard ad location can help build traffic for your business. Someone may see the ad, get interested in the offer, and reach out to you.

For an effective billboard ad, convey your brand message with imagery and text. The billboard should have a simple and interactive design with bold text against a contrasting color background. Make a creative ad message that is both interesting and memorable. Remember to include your business website or business phone number for client follow up.

One disadvantage of billboard advertising is that it can be quite costly. The cost of placing a billboard ad will depend on the location you choose, the amount of traffic in the location, and an estimated possible number of viewers. However, you will also have to pay for the board, branding, set up, and maintenance. Should the billboard structure be destroyed with disasters such as strong winds, you will have to pay for the repair cost.

Another disadvantage of this channel of advertising is that the targeted viewers are always on the move. It is, therefore, not easy for your potential borrowers to fully grasp the ad message.

You could also consider taking out an ad on the side of a city bus or on the bench or walls of a bus stop. This sort of advertising might reach your target customer, and they may have a little more time to see your ad. Contact an outdoor advertising specialist for details. One example of a national outdoor advertising company is Lamar http://www.lamar.com/. They have offices all over the United States and can answer any of your outdoor advertising needs.

Internet

Also referred to as digital advertising, online advertising is a cost-effective advertising channel and platform. Many people today have access to the internet and carry out their research online when looking for payday lenders.

One of the ways to carry out online advertising is through your website and investing in Search Engine Optimization (SEO) and affiliate marketing.

Social media and content marketing are other forms of online advertising.

Social Media Advertising

Social media is a low-cost advertising channel that can be used to create awareness and attract borrowers. Most adults have a social media account on either Facebook, Twitter, or Instagram. There is a high chance that your brand message will reach a potential borrower through these sites.

However, take note that Facebook and Google have placed restrictions on adverts for payday lenders and loans that attract an APR of 36% and above with less than 60 days' repayment period.

This advertising channel requires you to share important details of your loan business through blogs, videos, YouTube tutorials, or infographics. When potential borrowers find your content interesting, reliable, and trustworthy, they are likely to borrow from you.

Direct Marketing

This form of marketing is where you market directly to identified potential borrowers who are likely to take up loans from you. Posters, fliers, brochures, emails, phone calls, and text messages are cost-effective forms of direct marketing suitable for your business.

Design, print, and distribute the posters, flyers, and brochures to locations frequented by the identified potential customers. Personalize phone calls, text messages, and create enticing emails to individual potential clients.

What makes direct marketing effective is the fact that you send personalized messages to a specific target. Conversion rates associated with this kind of marketing is high as the targeted audience showed interest in your loans before the communication. You are also able to save on costs as direct marketing is targeted to specific individuals.

Some people, however, find this form of marketing to be intrusive and annoying. If your potential customers feel annoyed by, for example, your text messages, they could develop a negative perception towards your business.

Chapter 11: The Payday Loan Process from the Lender's Point of View

So far, we have discussed pretty much the entire establishment of a payday loan business. Early in this book, we looked at the payday lending process from the customer's side. Now, we need to look at the process from your side as the lender. What does selling a payday loan look like from the lender's point of view?

The reason you are in the payday loans business is to make money. To keep your business profitable, you need to determine the eligibility of your borrowers. Lending money to anyone who walks in without thoroughly screening them will soon lead to your business downfall. Keep it in mind that most of the payday loan borrowers are people who, for one reason or the other, do not qualify for loans from the bank. There is, therefore, a risk of non-repayment of the credit issued.

It is crucial that you decide on the methods you will use to determine customer eligibility before you start issuing loans. You can also consult your lawyer to make sure you have all you need for legal backing. With a strict loan policy, you stand to make significant profits. In this section, we shall discuss ways to determine borrower eligibility.

Basic Loan Requirements

A payday loan is meant to help the borrower meet an urgent financial need before their next payday. The payday loan, just as the name suggests, is a loan given against a post-dated check or authorization of account withdrawal on the borrower's next payday. The most basic requirements that the borrower needs to meet are:

- Proof of identification and that they are 18 years old and above, such as a State issued ID, Certificate of citizenship, Passport, Military ID, or Driver's license.

- An active bank account where you will deposit and even recover the loan. The duration they have been banking with the same bank can give you an indication of their financial stability.

- Proof of employment and reliable source of income; Employers contact information,

Previous three months' paystubs, Bank statements for the last three months, or a certified financial statement for the previous year (for the self-employed). To further prove that they are employed and have a source of income, you can request for their income tax returns and other supportive documents. Borrowers with fixed income make the best potential clients as you are sure their cash flow will be uninterrupted.

- An active phone number where you can reach them.

- Confirmation of residency through either a recent utility bill, rental agreement/contract, or references. Homeownership is an indication of some stability.

- Post-dated check or willingness to authorize account withdrawal.

Make copies of these documents and have in place procedures to keep them safe for future reference.

Bank Account Validation

Another way to determine borrower eligibility is by verifying the legitimacy of the bank account and statements that they give you. You can validate a bank account by calling the bank directly or through software programs such as Yodlee https://www.yodlee.com/ for account aggregation. These programs will provide you with read-only access to the bank account.

Creditworthiness

To make more profits, you may be tempted to offer as many loans as requested by a borrower. However, the question is whether they will pay it back. Determining a borrower's creditworthiness helps you gauge their likelihood of paying loans back. Creditworthiness is like a measurement tool used to measure the risk of lending to a client.

A low credit score means they are a high-risk borrower. A good or high credit rating, on the other hand, will give you the confidence that the client will make their repayment in full and on time. A first-time client with no borrowing history should be given a low credit score. You are not sure whether they will pay back on time or not. A repeat customer, on the other hand, is valuable. You already have a history with them, and you can expect that they will honor the loan repayment terms.

To determine a borrower's creditworthiness, request a copy of their credit report from a credit-reporting agency such as TransUnion, Equifax, and Experian.

Affordability Assessment

Affordability assessment involves establishing whether the borrower can afford to repay the loan within the contract terms. You must verify that the customer's monthly net salary can offset the loan amount they are seeking and still have some money left to take care of their necessary monthly expenses such as food and rent.

When carrying out bank account validation, you are given read-only access to the said account. This level of access enables you to check the borrower's income and withdrawal patterns. Use the incoming and outgoing financial information to determine the borrower's affordability of the loan they are requesting.

Financial Responsibility

In the case of a repeat customer, they need to show personal responsibility by paying off their previous debts to avoid an increasing debt level. It is risky to approve another loan until the previous debts are paid in full. Taking a loan to pay off another loan shows that the borrower is not financially organized.

Reason for Borrowing

Carry out a pre-loan interview to find out the client's reason and purpose of borrowing. Payday loans are for emergency needs or temporary financial shortfalls. Be wary of clients who borrow payday loans to use on long term projects such as constructing a house or for luxury purposes.

Honesty

Incomplete or inconsistent information filed in the loan application form should raise suspicion. Always double-check the information provided in the application form if it is consistent with what the client said during the pre-application interview. Incomplete sections of the form are an indication that they are either not sure what to write or are trying to hide something. Honesty is an essential factor to consider for the eligibility of a borrower.

However, some clients will not meet all the eligibility criteria. Some won't have a bank account or a job. Others will have a poor credit score. You can still choose to lend to them but with extra precautions. Below are ways to go about it.

A Borrower with No Active Bank Account

An active bank account presents an efficient and easy way to confirm that a borrower has a regular income and the source of that income. You will be able to find out if they are servicing other debts and whether they can afford to repay the loan they are seeking from you. You are also able to schedule your repayments through a standing order or a direct account debit to reduce the chances of non-repayment of a loan.

What do you do when a client comes for a payday loan, and they have no bank account? Do you turn them away? You can carry out a pre-loan interview to determine their reasons for not having a bank account. It is still possible to lend to such borrowers but consider them high risk and only give a small amount to minimize your loss in case of non-repayment. You can also charge them a slightly higher interest rate.

In this kind of situation, you or a company representative will have to go to the client's home to process and deliver the loan. You or the representative are thus the primary contact person regarding this loan. Henceforth, the contact person will be visiting the client's home on an agreed regular basis until the loan is repaid in full.

A Borrower with Bad Credit

Some borrowers have bad credit history emanating from either a late loan repayment or missing out a repayment. Borrowers with no history of borrowing can also have a low credit score. This kind of borrower is a high risk, but you can still extend to them a bad credit payday loan.

Bad credit payday loans are especially given to borrowers who are in an emergency or difficult financial situation but made mistakes in the past that negatively affected their credit ratings. The interest rates for this kind of payday loan is higher compared to what you would usually charge a borrower with a good or high credit score.

You can also consider asking the borrower to get a loan guarantor to back their application. The involvement of a guarantor reduces the perceived risk of lending to a client with bad credit. With a guarantor, you can offer the loan at better interest rates. The guarantor provides you with a second chance to get your loan repayment should the borrower fail to do so. However, the guarantor has to be someone with excellent credit history and meet all other payday loan eligibility requirements.

A Borrower Without Employment

Some people can carefully manage their finances and cover their daily needs, even when they are out of employment. However, emergencies and unexpected situations may arise and create an urgent or immediate need for extra money. When they are not able to quickly raise the needed amount, they may turn to payday loan lenders.

However, one of the basic requirements to qualify for a payday loan is proof of employment. You can still lend to such a client provided they can provide the following:

Proof of Good Credit History

The client should be able to show that in recent times, they have recorded no missed or late repayments and that they have been managing their debt responsibly.

Proof of Alternative Source of Income

Despite not being in employment, the borrower should provide you with some assurance that they will be able to repay the loan. Income doesn't always have to come from a monthly paycheck only. Other steady sources will suffice.

Pass Affordability Assessment

The client's alternative sources of income should be able to provide the borrower income that is sufficient to cover their regular basic needs and still have enough left to pay back the requested loan.

The other alternative sources of income that you can accept include proof of include:

- A running business or contract

- Unemployment benefits

- Social security payments

- Pension and retirement funds

- Disability income

- Child support payments

- Alimony

- Proceeds from a trust

- A cosigner

You could also consider proof that the borrower will access a significant amount of money in the near future, such as:

- An employment offer or contract

- A signed sale agreement of a real estate or investment property

- An inheritance they are about to receive

Treat such applications from borrowers with no employment with a lot of caution. To minimize your risk, you can approve a lower principal amount, enforce a shorter loan repayment duration, charge higher interest rates, or insist on an advance bank transfer approval.

Payday Loan Repayment Terms

The main aim of payday loans is to provide financial relief due to an emergency before a borrower's next payday. Payday loans are short-term loans, and the borrower is expected to make a full repayment from their next paycheck.

When a borrower is not able to pay back in time, the lender can agree to roll over the loan to the next month. The other option would be to allow the borrower to take out another loan to settle the previous one. When a borrower prolongs their repayment period, the lender could charge additional service fees or provide the second loan at a higher interest rate.

Conclusion

By now, I hope you feel like you're a wiz at the payday loans business. Of course, this book should not be your only source of information on the subject. I would strongly encourage you to enlist the help of an industry mentor or someone in person who has "been there, done that."

This book took you through the process of establishing your payday loan business from start-up to running the daily operations. We examined the reasons why you should enter into this business, as it's a business that is recession-proof and has been on the rise since the 1940s.

Payday loans offer a beneficial short-term personal lending solution that can really help many people make ends meet. Your business could be helping consumers right when they need it most. As long as you abide by the state and federal lending laws, your business will be viewed as reputable, and you'll be sure to have repeat business.

After reading this book, you will be well on your way to becoming an established pillar of business in your community.

Thank you for purchasing my book. If you would do me a huge favor and please consider leaving a review online where you made the purchase? Online reviews allow me to hear your feedback and, hopefully, will improve my future books. Reviews also help my work reach a wider audience. I would sincerely appreciate it, and thank you in advance.

www.ingramcontent.com/pod-product-compliance
Lightning Source LLC
Chambersburg PA
CBHW071357210526
45465CB00001B/136